At ✳ Issue

Is American Culture in Decline?

Auriana Ojeda, *Book Editor*

Bruce Glassman, *Vice President*
Bonnie Szumski, *Publisher*
Helen Cothran, *Managing Editor*

GREENHAVEN PRESS
An imprint of Thomson Gale, a part of The Thomson Corporation

THOMSON
✳ ™
GALE

Detroit • New York • San Francisco • San Diego • New Haven, Conn.
Waterville, Maine • London • Munich

Cover credits: © Digital Stock, Photos.com

LIBRARY OF CONGRESS CATALOGING-IN-PUBLICATION DATA

Is American culture in decline? / Auriana Ojeda, book editor.
    p. cm. — (At issue)
Includes bibliographical references and index.
ISBN 0-7377-2723-3 (lib. : alk. paper) — ISBN 0-7377-2724-1 (pbk. : alk. paper)
    1. United States—Moral conditions. 2. United States—Social conditions—
1980– . 3. United States—Politics and government—1989– . I. Ojeda, Auriana,
1977– . II. At issue (San Diego, Calif.)
HN90.M6I83 2005
306'.0973—dc22   2004054302

Printed in the United States of America

Contents

Introduction

A long-standing debate rages over the state of American culture, with critics lamenting the decline of the culture and supporters celebrating its improvement. Critic Paul Weyrich has stated, "The culture we are living in becomes an ever-wider sewer. In truth, I think we are caught up in a cultural collapse of historic proportions." Weyrich and others contend that increases in crime, drug abuse, broken homes, and ribald entertainment are reflective of a decline in American culture. Another critic, Jonathan Dolhenty, points out in his essay "Moral Mis-education and the Decline of American Culture" that since 1960 there has been a more than 400 percent increase in illegitimate births, a more than 200 percent increase in teen suicide rates, and a 560 percent increase in violent crime. "There is little question," he states, "that the cultural state of the nation is bad and getting worse. Society is indeed disintegrating; there are increases in drug abuse, alcohol abuse, child abuse, teen sexual activity, teen pregnancy, child and adult crime, venereal diseases . . . illegitimate children, single-parent households, divorce, and many antisocial behaviors."

However, others argue that Americans are behaving better today than they have for the last few decades. Even a few virtue watchdogs concede that Americans may be rising out of the immorality cesspool. The right-leaning monthly magazine *American Enterprise* warns fellow conservatives not to "accuse the American people of becoming morally rotten. Especially when there exist abundant data suggesting that the residents of our land are actually becoming less morally rotten." For example, David Whitman, senior writer for *U.S. News & World Report*, contends that fewer Americans today drink to excess, drink and drive, take drugs, or accept welfare than Americans did a quarter-century ago. In addition, more Americans engage in samaritan work with the poor, elderly, and ill, give more money to charity, and spend as much if not more time in church than in the past. Moreover, random violence is down, according to Whitman, as almost five hundred fewer people were murdered by strangers in 1997 than in 1977. The percentage of people who admit using drugs has dropped from 14.1 percent in 1979 to 6.4 percent in 1997. As Whitman notes, "If one looks beyond the anecdotes, the picture of how people behave is unexpectedly encouraging."

Some participants in the debate contend that the American family can be seen as the proverbial canary in the coal mine— its health is indicative of the state of American culture. According to William J. Bennett, former U.S. secretary of education and author of *The Broken Hearth: Reversing the Moral Collapse of the American Family*, the divorce rate has more than doubled, and out-of-wedlock births have skyrocketed since 1960. In addition, he points out, the percentage of single-parent families has more than tripled, the fertility rate has decreased, and the number of unmarried couples living together is almost eleven times greater than it was a few decades ago. Americans, Bennett writes,

> place less value than before on what we owe to others as a matter of moral obligation; less value on sacrifice as a moral good; less value on social conformity and respectability; and less value on correctness and restraint in matters of physical pleasure and sexuality.

According to Bennett and others, the disintegration of the family is directly related to the decline in American culture. As analyst George Roche states,

> The breakdown of the family—rather than poverty, race, or any other factor . . . is widely recognized now as the real root cause of rising rates of substance abuse, teen suicide, abortion, academic failure, welfare dependency, and violent crime.

Others argue that the American family is not on a path to total disintegration and is in fact growing stronger. According to Kay S. Hymowitz, contributing writer for *City Journal*, the divorce rate stabilized at its high of 50 percent and may even be declining. In addition, the number of children living with married parents rose from 68 percent in 1998 to 69 percent in 2002, the first upward movement in decades. Moreover, the number of African American children living with married parents rose from 34 percent in 1995 to 39 percent in 2000. Hymowitz concludes,

Today Americans are consciously, deliberately embracing ideas about sex, marriage, children, and the American dream that are coalescing into a viable . . . sort of bourgeois normality. What is emerging is a vital, optimistic, family-centered, entrepreneurial, and yes, morally thoughtful citizenry.

David Blankenhorn, president of the Institute for American Values, agrees that those trends are a positive sign. He writes, "These changes are not large or definitive. But they are certainly suggestive. And if they continue, they will change the lives of millions of American children and families for the better."

Some see in this apparent strengthening of the family hope for the future of American culture. Kay S. Hymowitz writes,

Americans have seen the damage that their decades-long fling with the sexual revolution and the transvaluation of traditional values wrought. And now, without giving up the real gains, they are earnestly knitting up their unraveled culture. It is a moment of tremendous promise.

As the controversy over the state of the American family illustrates, judging whether American culture is in decline is difficult and raises vital questions about the values Americans live by. These questions will continue to be debated as the country grows and changes.

1

America Shows Signs of a Moral Decline

John Harmon McElroy

John Harmon McElroy is a professor emeritus of English at the University of Arizona and the author of American Beliefs: What Keeps a Big Country and a Diverse People United, *from which the following viewpoint was excerpted.*

Since 1960 American culture has shown signs of decline. For example, marital infidelity and divorce are at an all-time high, more children are born out of wedlock than ever before, and abortions number about 1 million per year. Rates of crime and drug abuse have also increased. Moreover, standards of decency have fallen, as vulgar song lyrics, obscenity in the media, and burning the American flag are justified as "freedom of expression." These alarming trends, however, are increasingly criticized by social moralists, and many frightening statistics have leveled off. Indeed, the vast majority of Americans still believe that America is the "greatest nation on Earth," according to one poll. However, many American cultural beliefs, including the belief that "America is a chosen country," have weakened. Americans must unite to reclaim many of these cultural beliefs.

Americans believe in improvement, not decline. But should the formative and unifying set of beliefs that has been crucial to America's astonishingly rapid rise to prominence ever become deformed, the United States would surely decline. The past four decades [since 1960] have seen troubling signs of such cultural deformation.

Infidelity and Divorce

In no period of American history before the last forty years have families in every class of American society been so disrupted by marital infidelity and divorce (half of all American marriages now end in divorce), out-of-wedlock pregnancies (in 1963, 6.5 percent of Americans were born out of wedlock; in 1993, 30 percent), abortions (now averaging over one million a year) and new venereal diseases such as AIDS and herpes—the cumulative results of the "revolution" against "middle-class morality" on American campuses in the 1960s called the "counterculture," and the 1973 Supreme Court decision on abortion (*Roe v. Wade*). During these same forty years, federal courts across the land have been busy suppressing prayer in public schools and prohibiting the display of the Ten Commandments in public buildings. There has also been an unprecedented surge of drug abuse, the effects of which are now felt in every city, town, and rural community in America and in every class and age group. Criminal acts of many kinds have also risen to record levels and include such disturbing new features of life in America as killers under the age of twelve, recreational murder, and on-the-job and in-school multiple killings—all of which have necessitated record expenditures of public and private resources on personal security, uniformed police forces, and prison facilities.

> *The past four decades have seen troubling signs of . . . cultural deformation.*

The same period has likewise seen a growing disrespect for community standards of decency, reflected in speech patterns, obscenity in film and print media, violent song lyrics, and the burning of the American flag—all justified as nothing more than freedom of expression. And never before have so many Americans in all classes of society depended so heavily on government. (Taxes to support government spending now consume 40 percent of a typical American family's earnings. Put another way, the average American family works about three hours a day for tax collectors.) Still another basic change has occurred in public schooling in America: a shift of emphasis from teaching knowledge and skills to teaching "self-esteem"—

making it possible for some students to spend twelve years in the system and emerge functionally illiterate. A rewriting of American history as an uninterrupted tale of oppression and victimization has also occurred during these same forty years; and the idea of "multiculturalism" has entirely displaced America's national culture in the thinking of some Americans.

> **//** *Tolerance and choice . . . have been presented as values that override every other.* **//**

Since the mid-1960s, the growing reluctance of America's schools and universities to flunk students who are not measuring up to minimum standards of performance is part of a larger trend in American society: an unwillingness to pronounce any conduct as wrong. Americans have been made to feel in the past forty years that being "nonjudgmental" is a kind of higher morality. Tolerance and choice—*no matter what is tolerated or chosen*—have been presented as values that override every other. Sophistication, in the minds of too many Americans, has become a more important consideration than shame.

Positive Trends

As alarming as these symptoms of cultural decline may seem— and they are certainly alarming—they do not lead to the conclusion that American culture has yet been deformed. For one thing, most of the behavioral trends just cited are coming under increasingly heavy criticism, or have leveled off, or have been reversed. And some American beliefs, such as *Helping Others Helps Yourself* and *God Gave Men the Same Birthrights*, have actually been extended and strengthened since the 1960s. Most important, an overwhelming portion of the adult and young adult population of America still consists of responsible individuals.

For example, the Roper Center of Public Opinion Research in 1994 found that Americans across four generations (persons in their late teens to their late sixties and older) agreed that hard work is the key to getting ahead in America; that broadening opportunities is more important than ensuring equality of income; that big government is the greatest threat to America's future;

and that they were generally satisfied with their personal lives. Another national poll, taken in 1997, revealed that regardless of region, race, class, or age, most Americans still believe that "people have the power to shape their own lives, no matter what their circumstances, and that the best solutions are reached when people work together, cooperatively." Specifically in this poll, 83 percent agreed that "the USA is the greatest nation on Earth"; 95 percent that "freedom must be tempered by personal responsibility"; 89 percent that people have a "responsibility to help those less fortunate"; 79 percent that "people who work hard in this nation are likely to succeed"; and 81 percent that "a spiritual or religious belief is essential to a fulfilling life."

> *Americans must . . . recognize that many of their beliefs as a people have been weakened in the last four decades.*

Predictions of American decline have been made before and have proven false. And it is encouraging to remember that in the forty years from 1840 to 1880, which included a civil war, American beliefs survived. Cultures are tough. After all, cultural beliefs persist because they are durable.

Americans must nonetheless recognize that many of their beliefs as a people have been weakened in the last four decades, particularly the belief *America Is a Chosen Country*, which now seems to embarrass some Americans. (Had the 1997 poll that found an 83 percent agreement that "the USA is the greatest nation on Earth" been taken in 1957, I suspect the percentage of agreement would have been somewhere above 90.) Other American beliefs which—though still strong—have been somewhat diminished are the religious and moral beliefs *God Created Nature and Human Beings, God Created a Law of Right and Wrong*, and *Doing What Is Right Is Necessary for Happiness;* the social and economic beliefs *Everyone Must Work, Society Is a Collection of Individuals, Each Person Is Responsible for His Own Well-Being*, and *Opportunities Must Be Imagined* (as opposed to being provided by the government); the political beliefs *A Majority Decides* and *The Least Government Possible Is Best;* and the belief about human nature *Human Beings Will Abuse Power When They Have It* (whose weakening is suggested by judicial decisions nullifying state laws to limit the number of terms of elected representatives).

The end result of the simultaneous weakening of so many American beliefs has been to alter the dynamics of American culture. To account for how and why these beliefs have been weakened is beyond the scope of this [writing], but it is certain that since World War II some principles of American culture have been emphasized to the detriment of others. The principle of freedom, for instance, has been promoted without regard to responsibility; calls for improvement have been made without regard to practicality; and equality has sometimes been demanded with a zeal that ignores differences among individuals. Too often in the last forty years of the twentieth century, it seems, America's cultural history has been set aside in favor of uncompromising ideologies.

As always, America's future depends on the unity of the American people, just as George Washington said it did in his Farewell Address in 1796, three years before his death. And that unity is, as always, mostly a matter of the beliefs that Americans share and act on as a people.

2

American Culture Is Not in Decline

Kay S. Hymowitz

Kay S. Hymowitz is a senior fellow at the Manhattan Institute and a contributing editor of City Journal. *She writes extensively on education and childhood in America. Hymowitz has also written for many major publications including the* New York Times, *the* Washington Post, *the* Wall Street Journal, *the* New Republic, New York Newsday, *the* Public Interest, Commentary, Dissent, *and* Tikkun.

The new generation of kids is turning away from the destructive aspects of the culture that developed in the 1960s. They are performing better in school, having less sex, and doing fewer drugs than teenagers were ten years ago. Teen crime rates have also decreased. More teens are getting along with their parents, and even more have a positive view of marriage in spite of the high divorce rate. More people support the nuclear family today than in the past thirty years. Despite the trends, Americans still revel in the post–sexual revolution culture, as depicted in bawdy films such as *American Pie*, in which a group of boys try to lose their virginity before high school graduation. Thus, Americans are striving to undo some of the damage caused by an era that dismissed traditional values without giving up the freedoms the culture has gained.

S ex doesn't sell: Miss Prim is in. No, editors at the *New York Times* "Sunday Styles" section were not off their meds when they came up with that headline recently. Just think about some of the Oscar nominees this year [2004]: there was *Seabiscuit,* a classic inspirational story of steadfast outsiders beating huge odds to win the race; *Return of the King: Lord of the Rings,* a mythic battle of good defeating evil, featuring female characters as pure as driven snow; *Master and Commander,* a nineteenth-century naval epic celebrating courage, discipline, and patriarchal authority. And then there was *Lost in Translation,* in which a man in the throes of a midlife crisis spends hours in a hotel room with a luscious young woman, and . . . they talk a lot.

If you listen carefully, you can hear something shifting deep beneath the manic surface of American culture. Rap stars have taken to wearing designer suits. Miranda Hobbs, *Sex and the City's* redhead, has abandoned hooking up and a Manhattan co-op for a husband and a Brooklyn fixer-upper, where she helps tend her baby and ailing mother-in-law; even nympho Samantha has found a "meaningful relationship." Madonna is writing children's books. Gloria Steinem is an old married lady.

> *Americans have been self-correcting from a decades-long experiment with 'alternative values.'*

Yessiree, family values are hot! Capitalism is cool! Seven-grain bread is so yesterday, and red meat is back!

Wave away the colored smoke of the Jackson family circus, Paris Hilton, and the antics of San Francisco,[1] and you can see how Americans have been self-correcting from a decades-long experiment with "alternative values." Slowly, almost imperceptibly during the 1990s, the culture began a lumbering, Titanic turn away from the iceberg, a movement reinforced by the 1990s economic boom and the shock of the 9/11 terrorist attacks. [Since 1994] most of the miserable trends in crime, divorce, illegitimacy, drug use, and the like that we saw in the decades after

---

1. In 2004, Michael Jackson was accused for the second time of molesting a young boy, and Janet Jackson was harshly criticized for exposing her breast at the Super Bowl half-time performance. Socialite Paris Hilton, of the Hilton hotel fortune, was humiliated when a video depicting her having sex circulated the Internet. San Francisco became the first city in 2004 to issue marriage licenses to gay couples; the Supreme Court ordered the city to stop issuing licenses to gay couples in March 2004. In May 2004, Massachusetts became the first state to allow gay couples to legally wed.

1965 either turned around or stalled. Today Americans are consciously, deliberately embracing ideas about sex, marriage, children, and the American dream that are coalescing into a viable—though admittedly much altered—sort of bourgeois normality. What is emerging is a vital, optimistic, family-centered, entrepreneurial, and yes, morally thoughtful, citizenry.

The Kids Are All Right

To check a culture's pulse, first look at the kids, as good a crystal ball as we have. Yes, there's reason to worry: guns in the schools, drugs, binge drinking, cheating, Ritalin, gangs, bullies, depression, oral sex, Internet porn, you name it. Kids dress like streetwalkers and thugs, they're too fat, they don't read, they watch too much television, they never play outside, they can't pay attention, they curse like *South Park*'s Eric Cartman. The 1950s, this ain't.

Yet marketers who plumb people's attitudes to predict trends are noticing something interesting about "Millennials," the term that generation researchers Neil Howe and William Strauss invented for the cohort of kids born between 1981 and 1999: they're looking more like Jimmy Stewart than James Dean. They adore their parents, they want to succeed, they're optimistic, trusting, cooperative, dutiful, and civic-minded. "They're going to 'rebel' by being, not worse, but better," write Howe and Strauss.

> *The U.S. is the only country that saw a dramatic drop in teen pregnancy during the last decade.*

However counterintuitive, there's plenty of hard evidence to support this view. Consider the most basic indicator of social health: crime. The juvenile murder rate plummeted 70 percent between 1993 and 2001. By 2001, the arrest rate for all violent crime among juveniles was down 44 percent from its 1994 peak, reaching its lowest level since 1983. Juvenile arrests for burglary were also down 66 percent in that time period. Vandalism is at its lowest level in two decades. Despite all the headlines to the contrary, schools are a lot safer: school-based crimes dropped by close to half in the late 1990s. According to the Youth Risk Behavior Survey, the percentage of ninth- through 12th-graders who reported being in a fight anywhere in the previous 12 months dropped from 42 percent in 1991 to 33 percent in 2001, while those who had been in a fight on school property fell from 16 percent to 13 percent.

> *Poll after poll depicts a generation that thinks their parents are just grand.*

Something similar looks like it may be happening with adolescent drinking and drug use, on the rise throughout much of the nineties. But suddenly, around the turn of the millennium, the nation's teens started to climb back on the wagon. Monitoring the Future, an annual University of Michigan survey of the attitudes and behavior of high school students, reports that by 2002 the percentage of kids who reported binge drinking in the last 30 days was close to its lowest level in the 12 years that the survey has been following eighth- and tenth-graders and in the 30 years that it has been following high school seniors. Though during the 1990s marijuana use rose sharply among eighth-graders and less dramatically among tenth- and 12th-graders, by late in the decade the numbers began to fall. More broadly, the Department of Health and Human Services reports that all illicit teen drug use dropped 11 percent between 2001 and 2003. Ecstasy use, which soared between 1998 and 2001, fell by more than half among high schoolers. A 2003 National Center on Addiction and Substance Abuse study found that 56 percent of teenagers have no friends who drink regularly, up from 52 percent in 2002, and 68 percent say they have no friends using marijuana, up from 62 percent—even though 40 percent of them say they would have no trouble finding the stuff if they wanted it. They're just not interested.

Just Saying No

And what about teen sex? Only yesterday, you'd have thought there was no way to wrangle that *horse* back into the barn. No more. According to the Alan Guttmacher Institute, out-of-wedlock teen pregnancy rates have come down 28 percent from their high in 1990, from a peak of 117 per thousand girls ages 15 to 19 to 83.6 per thousand in 2000. The teen abortion rate also fell—by a third—during the same period. True, American kids still get pregnant at higher rates than those in other major Western nations, but the U.S. is the only country that saw a dramatic drop in teen pregnancy during the last decade.

While American kids are more often saying yes to birth control, even more of them, remarkably, are just saying no to sex, just as they are passing up marijuana and beer. According to the 1991 Youth Risk Behavior Survey, 54 percent of teens reported having had sex; a decade later, the number was 46 percent. The number of high schoolers who reported four or more partners also fell from 18.7 percent to 14.2 percent.

> *Americans . . . are marriage nuts.*

Making the decline in sexual activity more striking is that it began just around the same time that Depo-Provera, a four-shots-a-year birth control technology specifically aimed at teens, came on the market. It's often been said that the birth control pill, which became available to the public in the early 1960s, propelled the sexual revolution. The lesson of Depo-Provera, which was accompanied by a decrease in sexual activity, is that it isn't technology that changes sexual behavior. It's the culture. . . .

Happy Families

Look, for instance, at what's happening to teen alienation. If Millennials have a problem with authority, it's that they wish they had *more* of it. Poll after poll depicts a generation that thinks their parents are just grand. A 2003 *American Demographics* survey shows 67 percent of teens "give Mom an A." They tell interviewers for the National Campaign to Prevent Teen Pregnancy that they want *more* advice about sex from their parents. Summarizing opinion polls, researcher Neil Howe says that this generation is at least as attached to their parents and their values as any generation before. "When it comes to 'Do you get along with your family?' it's never been as high. Same thing for 'Do you believe in the values of your parents?' When they're asked 'Do you trust your parents to help you with important life decisions?' they don't see parents as meddling or interfering," Howe concludes. "They're grateful."

> *The divorce rate . . . is certainly stabilizing, and possibly even declining.*

In fact, when it comes to families, this generation is as mushy as a Hallmark card. A Harris Interactive survey of college seniors found that 81 percent planned to marry (12 percent already had) at a mean age of 28. Ninety-one percent hope to have children—and get this: on average, they'd like to have *three*. The 2001 Monitoring the Future survey found 88 percent of male high school seniors and 93 percent of females believing that it is extremely or quite important to have a good marriage and family life. In a survey of college women conducted by the Institute for American Values, 83 percent said, "Being married is a very important goal for me." Over half of the women surveyed said they would like to meet their husbands in college.

What makes this marriage schmaltziness so striking, of course, is that it's coming from people who grew up when that institution was in tatters. For a lot of culture watchers, nothing brings out the inner Cassandra[2] more than the state of marriage—and for good reason, especially when you shift your focus from the young to the entire population. The divorce rate hovers near 50 percent. A third of all babies are born to unmarried mothers, a number considerably higher for black babies. The proportion of never-married women between the ages of 30 and 39 has almost tripled in the last 30 years. Laura Kipnis, author of the recent plaint *Against Love: A Polemic*, only seemed to be saying the obvious in her January [2004] *New York Times* op ed: "More and more people—heterosexuals that is—don't want to get or stay married these days, no matter their income level." After all, Kipnis continued, quoting numbers that are a favorite of contemporary marriage "realists," "only 56 percent of all adults are married, compared with 75 percent 30 years ago. The proportion of traditional married-couple-with-children American households has dropped to 26 percent of all

---

2. Cassandra was a Greek goddess known for predicting disastrous events.

households, from 45 percent in the early 1970's."

Except the obvious is wrong. Americans—particularly younger Americans at or approaching marriageable age—are marriage nuts. They meditate endlessly on the subject. Having put aside sitcoms about latte-drinking hook-up athletes—*Seinfeld* has died and gone to rerun heaven—they watch reality shows like *The Bachelor, The Bachelorette, The Littlest Groom, Average Joe,* and *Trista and Ryan's Wedding,* and movies like *My Big Fat Greek Wedding.* On *Friends,* the space cadet Phoebe just had a white-dress wedding, while Monica and Chandler are married, adopting a baby, and moving to the burbs. In real life, the number of married-couple families, after declining in the seventies and eighties, rose 5.7 percent in the nineties, according to demographer William H. Frey.

And in fact, the incredible shrinking married-couple-with-children statistic cited by Kipnis is a statistical mirage, an artifact of two demographic trends, unconnected with American attitudes toward knot tying. First, young people are marrying later; the average age is 25 for women, 27 for men, up from 20 and 23 three decades ago. That means there are a lot more young singles out there than there were in 1970. Further swelling the ranks of these un–Ozzies and Harriets is the vastly increased number of empty nesters, retirees, and widows, beneficiaries of major health-care improvements over the past decades. There are 34 million Americans over 65, and it's a safe bet that only those few living with their adult kids would be counted as part of a married-couple household with children. What it comes down to is that a smaller proportion of married couples with children is no more evidence of the decline of the family than more cars on the road is evidence of a decline in trucks.

Bringing Back the Family

Even on the fraught issue of out-of-wedlock births and divorce, there are grounds for hope. In the population at large, the decades-long trend toward family fragmentation has finally halted and, according to some numbers, is even reversing itself. Overall, the proportion of children in married-parent families rose from 68 percent in 1998 to 69 percent in 2002—a tiny boost, to be sure, but the first upward tick in decades. More encouragingly, after plummeting between 1965 and 1992, the number of black children living with married parents rose from 34 percent in 1995 to 39 percent in 2000. Moreover, the longitudinal Fragile Families and Child Wellbeing Study has found that half of the poor, largely black, new mothers it surveys are living with the father at the time of their baby's birth. Two-thirds of them agree "it is better for children if their parents are married," and 77 percent say that chances of marrying their child's father are 50 percent or higher. If history is any guide, most won't; but the fact that so many want to marry and understand that it is better to do so is an unexpected bit of social capital to build on.

> *An edgy exterior no longer necessarily connotes a radical life-style.*

Americans are even beginning to look at divorce with a more jaded eye. The divorce rate—statistically hard to pin down—is certainly stabilizing, and possibly even declining from its record high of 50 percent. Not so long ago, orthodox opinion would natter on about marital breakup as an opportunity for adults' "personal growth" or about "resilient children" who were "better off when their parents were happy." For the children of divorce who are now in their childbearing years, such sunny talk grates. They saw their mothers forced to move to one-bedroom apartments while their fathers went off with new girlfriends; they found out what it was like when your father moved from being the love object who read to you every night, to a guy who lives across the country whom you see once a year. When it comes to marriage and children, a lot of these damaged young adults are determined to do better. Nic Carothers, the 18-year-old son of divorced parents interviewed by the *Indianapolis Star*, explained his determination to avoid sex until he marries for life: "My father wasn't a very responsible man. I want to be a better father when the time is right." "I can't tell you how many 30-somethings are still in therapy because of their parents' divorce," Catherine Stellin, of Youth Intelligence, told me. "Now we're hearing that maybe it's a good thing to stay together for the sake of the kids."

This change of view is not limited to the heartland. Writing in the mainstream *Atlantic Monthly*, Caitlin Flanagan recently offered mild praise for *The Proper Care & Feeding of Husbands*, by much reviled talk-show host Dr. Laura: "There are many of us who understand that once you have children, certain doors ought to be closed to you forever. That to do right by a child means more than buying the latest bicycle helmet and getting him on the best soccer team. . . . It means investing oneself completely in the marriage that wrought him." Flanagan went on to chastise feminist male-bashing. "Our culture is quick to point out the responsibilities husbands have to wives—they should help out with the housework, be better listeners, understand that a woman wants to be more than somebody's mother and somebody's wife—but very reluctant to suggest that a wife has a responsibility to a husband." Such views didn't sink Flanagan's career; she will now be publishing her marriage-happy essays in the *bien-pensant New Yorker.*

In fact, applause for the nuclear family is now coming even from the American academy and from left-leaning advocacy groups. For decades, elites jeered at the assumption that changes in family structure would harm children; remember the guffaws that greeted Vice President Dan Quayle's pro-marriage *Murphy Brown* speech[3] in 1992? But by the 1990s, study after study began showing, as Barbara Dafoe Whitehead put it in a landmark 1993 *Atlantic Monthly* article, that "Dan Quayle Was Right"—that, on average, children in married, two-parent families do better than other kids by every measure of success. Once-skeptical experts began acknowledging that the traditionalists had it right all along, and advocates announced, in the words of ChildTrends, that "[m]arriage is one of the most beneficial resources for adults and children." Just a decade ago it seemed impossible to imagine a leftish organization like the Center for Law and Social Policy going on record that "society should try to help more children grow up with their two biological, married parents in a reasonably healthy, stable relationship," but that's what has happened. . . .

Bourgeois Booty-Shakers

Even after all these changes, of course, we still live in a post–sexual revolution culture. Nobody pretends we're going back to the 1950s. Americans may have abandoned the credo of "if it feels good, do it," but they still embrace sexual pleasure as a great human good and take pride in advertising their own po-

---

3. In 1992 then–vice president Dan Quayle criticized television's Murphy Brown for having a child out of wedlock.

tential for success in that area. David Brooks coined the term "bobo" to refer to bourgeois bohemians, but the newest generation of bobos might be better described as bourgeois booty-shakers. Young mothers go to "strip aerobics" classes, where they do their workout by pole dancing, before they go off to pick up little Tiffany at kindergarten. Madonna does some provocative tongue wrestling with Britney Spears on national television, but everyone knows that in reality she glories in being a Hollywood soccer mom (and Mrs. Guy Ritchie, as she would have it). An edgy exterior no longer necessarily connotes a radical life-style: not long ago, I watched a heavily pierced couple, as the bride-to-be, with her stringy, dyed red hair, torn jeans, and bright green sneakers, squealed over the pear-shaped diamond engagement ring she was trying on. Go figure.

> **❝** *The public has its own mind, influenced by forces more powerful than the television or movie screen.* **❞**

The popular media has been trying to make sense of these crosscurrents. Some writers seem to grasp that they can bombard their viewers with breast and fart jokes, but in the end people are still interested in how to live meaningful lives. Consider the WB network's popular series *Gilmore Girls*. The main character, Lorelai Gilmore, is a single 30-something who had a baby when she was 16. A motor-mouthed girl-woman, she picks fights with her now-teenage daughter over the size of their "boobs," makes pop-culture allusions as obsessively as any teenybopper, and mugs and pouts during her weekly adolescent-style tiffs with her own parents. The daughter, Rory, on the other hand, is the proto-Millennial: sober, hardworking, respectful, and chaste. Her hell-raiser mother's jaw drops when she hears that her daughter hasn't really thought about having sex with her boyfriend. Meanwhile, this season Rory is a freshman at Yale, where she writes for the school paper and reads, you know, literature. (*The Sun Also Rises*? On the network that gave us *Dawson's Creek*?) Yes, this is a piece of pop-culture effluvium, but its point, made weekly, is that Rory has the promising future, while her mother reflects the childish past.

Look also at *American Wedding* [2003] sequel to the movie

American Pie, a foul teen cult film about a group of high school boys determined to have sex before they graduate. (On second thought, don't—unless your idea of cinematic fun includes extended jokes about pubic hair and dog doo.) In one scene of the sequel, which depicts the nuptials of one of the couples that we met in the earlier movie, the bride-to-be, Michelle, asks her future father-in-law to help her write her vows. "How do you describe making love?" he asks her, to get her started on her composition. But Michelle can only think of vulgarisms: she stands for a generation that, like Shakespeare's Caliban [a character in *The Tempest*], has yet to be taught a civilized language. Still, her wedding, complete with white gown, bridesmaids, toasts, and a band that plays fox trots, clearly reflects her longing for the sort of refined feelings that she has no words for. "How did a perv like you become such a great guy?" Michelle asks her new husband, after she delivers her vows, marked by their sincerity if not their poetry, during "the wedding of her dreams." "How did a nympho like you become such a great girl?" he asks her in turn. It is a wonder.

A New Seriousness

And that surprise takes us back to the most vexing issue of our day: gay marriage, which encapsulates the tension between the sexual revolution and the new conventionality. On the one hand, it asserts the value of unrestrained sexual desire; on the other, it celebrates our new seriousness about constructing traditional meaning, solidity, and connection out of those desires in a vulgar and rootless post-liberation landscape. Regardless of how Americans resolve this tension, the change in the cultural zeitgeist means that, for all their wealth and fame, the Quentin Tarantinos and Ice Ts of this culture do not own it. The public has its own mind, influenced by forces more powerful than the television or movie screen. The purveyors of fashion and entertainment try to decipher the cultural mood.

So, the latest ads for Gucci leave sexual decadence behind for mystery and romance. Why? Because these trendsetters sense something new. "What we did was sort of instinctual. We just felt there was something in the air," Doug Lloyd, one of Gucci's admen, told the *New York Times*. "Believe it or not, I am a little sick of blatant sexual poses in advertising," Gucci designer Tom Ford, a man who once had a G shaved into a model's crotch and hired a photographer to snap the results, told

Harper's Bazaar. So Abercrombie and Fitch canceled their Christmas catalog after the outcry over its orgy tips for teens. So Viacom president Mel Karmazin chided his radio stations: "This company won't be a poster child for indecency." More surprising than Janet Jackson's breast reveal was the vigorous public spanking that she and Justin Timberlake received after it was over. For what it's worth, my 16-year-old daughter tells me that the girls she knows with pierced navels now see them as "skanky" and wish they could undo them. Now they care about SEXY TOPS THAT DON'T LOOK TRASHY, as a recent *Seventeen* headline promised to explain to its teen readers.

With their genius for problem solving and compromise, pragmatic Americans have seen the damage that their decades-long fling with the sexual revolution and the transvaluation of traditional values wrought. And now, without giving up the real gains, they are earnestly knitting up their unraveled culture. It is a moment of tremendous promise.

3

Popular Culture Contributes to America's Decline

Richard Alleva

Richard Alleva is a film critic for Commonweal *magazine and a contributor to* Image *magazine.*

In 1896 William Butler Yeats commented that Alfred Jarry's comedic play *King Ubu* stretched the limits of tasteful comedy with its use of scatological humor. In the last several decades, popular culture has sunk to new lows with the rise of magazines such as *Mad* and *National Lampoon*, both of which are known for their satirical bathroom humor. In addition, popular icons, such as rap star Eminem and so-called shock jocks, have risen to fame largely because of their unprecedented vulgarity. This rise of sordid entertainment is due in part to an attitude that developed among young people in the Vietnam War era to reject the war-ravaged world created by their elders and revert to the humor of their childhood—the "sick" humor exemplified by *Mad* magazine. Since that time, entertainers have sought fame by pushing the boundaries of vulgarity. The most obscene acts are now the most popular ones.

In Paris, on December 11, 1896, William Butler Yeats attended the opening night of a play. Years later, he wrote about the event in his autobiography.

> I go to the first performance of Jarry's *Ubu Roi* [*King Ubu*], at the Theatre de l'Oeuvre. . . . The audience

shake their fists at one another. . . . The players are supposed to be dolls, toys, marionettes, and now they are all hopping like wooden frogs, and I can see for myself that the chief personage, who is some kind of king, carries for a scepter a brush of the kind that we use to clean a closet. Feeling bound to support the most spirited party, we have shouted for the play, but that night . . . I am very sad, for comedy, objectivity, has displayed its growing power once more. . . . After S. Mallarme, after Verlaine . . . after our own verse, after the faint mixed tints of Condor [sic], what more is possible? After us, the Savage God.

Despite his limited knowledge of French, Yeats well understood that he was seeing no ordinary comedy but something raw and unleashed, something that tore aside artfully arranged veils and wiped away the "faint mixed tints" not only of a painter like Charles Conder but of everything impressionistic, including the Celtic twilight of his own early verse. *King Ubu*, based on the playwright Alfred Jarry's own physics teacher at his lycee, is a grotesque exaggeration of the classic tragic tyrant, a Macbeth transformed into a screaming puppet. He wields a toilet brush as scepter, carries his conscience about in a suitcase, and the very first word he utters on stage is a deliberate misspelling of the French for excrement.

A Peculiar Savagery

There is satire in the play, but satire—mockery of evil and stupidity in defense of virtue and competence—is never its main objective. Ubu serving excrement at his royal feast, with his wife responding "chacun a son gout"[1] to a guest's mild objection; the tyrant taking oaths "by my green candle," meaning his own gonorrheic sex organ; he and his wife squabbling in the language of two kids slanging each other in a schoolyard; the king slaughtering his entire bureaucracy by dropping each official through a trap-door into a dungeon where they will be "debrained"—all this serves a comedy that strips mankind of all striving for dignity, conscience, sentiment. This is the peculiar savagery of the Savage God.

---

1. French phrase that translates as, "Each person to his (own) taste"

As Roger Shattuck wrote in *The Banquet Years* (1977), "The schoolboy imagination had succeeded in throwing dung in the public eye. Some laughed and some were incensed, but no one could deny that it had been cunningly thrown. . . . One must be careful not to look for the psychological veracity of satire in his [Jarry's] writing. He did not proceed like [other comedic writers] Molière or Aristophanes or Mark Twain, in whose works we find an intensification of familiar human characteristics. Jarry's humor may rather be regarded as a psychological refusal to repress distasteful images. He laughed and invited us to laugh at Ubu's most monstrous behavior . . . because it is a means of domesticating fear and pain."

> *King Ubu . . . is a grotesque exaggeration of the classic tragic tyrant.*

In 1906, Jarry's writings established the farthest outposts of the literary avant-garde. But now, a century later, the Savage God has a townhouse in Manhattan and a ranch house in the suburbs. He's no longer a ragtag bohemian but a middle-class swell. The avant-garde of yesterday is today's pop culture, and much of that pop culture is notably in debt to the style of *King Ubu*.

Consider his progeny:

• The "shock jocks" of radio with their bathroom humor and insulting phone calls.

• Many "Saturday Night Live" skits, such as the one that pretends to be an advertisement for a device that transforms flatulence into human speech, thus allowing the victims of public gastric attacks to pretend to be making offhand comments.

• The "South Park" TV series and movie.

• A large portion of the monologues of late-night TV hosts, especially Jay Leno.

• Many currently popular comedies, with *There's Something about Mary* leading the pack.

• *National Lampoon* magazine, which has always fastened, with a child's horrified fascination, on death, disease, and decay for much of its humor. Since many of *Lampoon*'s alumni went to work on TV shows such as "SNL" and "Mad TV," and the former's movie spinoffs, Ubuesque humor was dispersed throughout the culture.

• Since Ubu and his descendants drew upon a childish out-
look while perpetrating their humor, it should come as no surprise that several of today's children's films now channel childish toilet jokes right back to the kids. Kiddie moviemaking,
once squeaky-clean, is now pretty raunchy. *Shrek* and *The Em-
peror's New Groove* are a long way from *Bambi*, both in their hip-
ness and in their grossness.

• Eminem has less in common with other rappers than
with Quentin Tarantino, Lenny Bruce (at his most extreme),
the Robert Smigel cartoons featured on "Saturday Night Live,"
the horror comics of the 1950s, and the early films of Sam
Raimi (for example, *The Evil Dead*). Good or bad, Mr. Marshall
Mathers (AKA Eminem) has found his form: not the rap song
but the aural skit, very close to radio drama. In fact, listening
to an Eminem number such as "Bonnie and Clyde 97" is like
hearing one of the old radio melodramas, "Lights Out" or "Cli-
max," rewritten by a psycho.

Seeking Explanations

How and why did it happen? How did America, the most culturally puritanical nation in the Western world, become the
most ribald and assaultive of entertainment purveyors? And
why did it happen so fast, in only the last thirty-five years or so?

> *How did America, the most culturally
> puritanical nation in the Western world, become
> the most ribald and assaultive of entertainment
> purveyors?*

First: How? To be sure, American writers and entertainers
didn't all suddenly begin reading Alfred Jarry and decide to become his epigones. Many of the entertainers I've mentioned
may never have heard of Ubu, much less read it. But Jarry's
writings influenced those of Apollinaire, Andre Breton, and
Roger Vitrac, and eventually, at the end of a long chain of sur-
realists, those of Eugene Ionesco and Samuel Beckett. Their
plays crossed the Atlantic and were extensively performed in
the 1950s and '60s in New York venues and by university and
repertory theaters throughout the country during a short but

intense period which gave rise to the label, Theater of the Absurd. The texts of Jarry, Beckett, and Ionesco became the assigned reading of drama and comparative literature courses, and their influence was felt in the early plays of Edward Albee (*The Sand Box*), Arthur Kopit (*Oh Dad, Poor Dad, Mamma's Hung You in the Closet and I'm Feelin' So Sad*), and several others.

> *Once you have domesticated one aspect of fear and pain, you must move on to another.*

Simultaneously, and perhaps more important, kids of the 1950s, '60s, and early '70s were being culturally nourished (or malnourished) on the magazines *Mad, Cracked,* and *Sick,* on Steve Allen, the American version of the British TV show, "That Was the Week that Was," horror comic books, Loony Tunes cartoons, Soupy Sales, the Three Stooges, "The Adventures of Rocky and Bullwinkle," and on a host of other pop entities that suggested a view of life not far removed from Theater of the Absurd. The more intellectual kids were also listening to the records of Lenny Bruce, Shelly Berman, and Nichols and May, and maybe reading Allen Ginsberg, William Burroughs, and Terry Southern. Sooner or later—and in America everything happens sooner—the angst celebrated by highbrow culture and the raucousness of pop culture had to merge, and the angst, energized by the raucousness, would begin to look more and more like a slap-happy, devil-may-care nihilism.

What we are seeing and hearing now in American pop culture are the offspring of an intellectually mixed marriage: the children of the French avant-garde and all-American nuttiness. Jarry/Ionesco/Beckett has mated with Bugs Bunny/*Mad* magazine/Bullwinkle the Moose, and their offspring turns out to be "South Park." Ubuesque nuttiness prevailed but with a rock 'n' roll beat.

A Childhood Culture

But why did it all come together and flourish around 1970?

At the end of the sixties, a great number of young people were confronting the possibility of early death in the Vietnam War and entertaining a ferocious contempt for what they took to be the corruption of the society that launched America into that war. The civil strife of generations produced a tendency among the young to turn away from an adult world "we never made." And this revulsion prompted an elevation of certain strains of childhood culture, not the least of them the "sick humor of the fifties." The Vietnam War finally ended and the civil war of generations was abraded by the passing of years, but the sick comedy strain was here to stay, and this strain has been more than a coloration of our recent bawdy pop culture. It is very nearly its ethos.

But why did all become so nasty in the last few years, so raucous, so mephitic? Even Jarry himself might be a bit shocked by Eminem and turn up his nose at "South Park."

Look again at that quote from Roger Shattuck. He writes of Jarry's obscenity and humor being a way of domesticating fear and pain. Yes, but once you have domesticated one aspect of fear and pain, you must move on to another. You must find a new nerve to hit, a new outrage to perpetrate. You must turn up the volume, find a new blasphemy to utter, discover the certain something still unsayable that you, and you alone, dare to say. Put purple blood in the next slaughter, crack a joke about child rape, suggest that necrophilia is just a matter of taste. Now, combine this need with the recent economic hypertrophy (we can't make just millions, it must be billions, or what will we say to our stockholders?) and you have a pretty reliable forecast of the future: Louder! Meaner! Nastier!

King Ubu has been surpassed but King Ubu still rules.

4

Popular Culture Does Not Contribute to America's Decline

Tyler Cowen

Tyler Cowen is a professor of economics at George Mason University and the author of Creative Destruction: How Globalization Is Changing the World's Cultures *and* In Praise of Commercial Culture.

Modern culture supports the arts as no previous culture has. Technological and commercial innovations have brought music of all kinds, including classical, popular, and international, into nearly all parts of the world. Films, including classics and silent, are readily available for rent or purchase. Rather than killing the printed word, television and the Internet have stimulated interest in books, which are now available in every genre imaginable. In addition, many new artistic media have sprung up, including cable television, the Web, and virtual reality technology. Moreover, other artistic endeavors, such as fashion, cuisine, and computer graphics, are blossoming. These cultural innovations have flourished because of America's wealthy capitalist society. However, many cultural pessimists criticize modern popular culture in favor of historical achievements. Their mistake is comparing the very best accomplishments of past cultures with the entirety of modern culture, which is bound to produce some trashy work. Critics have been lamenting the decline of culture for centuries, not recognizing that the works they attack today are sometimes considered masterpieces in the future.

The music of Johann Sebastian Bach, Wolfgang Amadeus Mozart, Joseph Haydn, and Ludwig van Beethoven is more accessible to today's listeners than to those of the 18th or 19th centuries. Modern concertgoers can sample an unparalleled range of musical periods, instruments, and styles. Even relatively obscure composers' material is stocked in music superstores, the largest of which carry up to 22,000 titles. One company label markets excellent performances of the classics for as little as $5.99 for 70 minutes of music. Music of all kinds—old and new—is available in great profusion.

> *Television, video stores, and bookstores give modern fans better access to the works of Shakespeare than the Elizabethans had.*

Movies, including many silents, can be rented or purchased on videocassettes, or on DVDs for those who want higher-quality picture and sound. Modern video stores, run on a private for-profit basis, are libraries full of classic films.

New and definitive editions of many literary works, or better translations, are published regularly. The Bible and Plato, two favorites of many cultural pessimists, continue to be reissued in new editions, while many of the classics are available in paperback. Television, video stores, and bookstores give modern fans better access to the works of Shakespeare than the Elizabethans had.

Positive Trends

Literacy and reading are two areas where the modern world comes in for especially harsh criticism, but even here the trends are largely positive. American illiteracy was far worse 100 years ago or even in the middle of the 20th century. Furthermore, the average American buys more than twice as many books today as in 1947. The number of bookstores has jumped nearly tenfold, and their average size has increased dramatically. Book superstores have become commonplace.

Contrary to the many claims, television and the Internet are not killing the book. The printed word offers unique modes of story-telling and analysis that other media have not replaced. Television and the Internet often complement reading and stimulate reader interest . . . books, rather than replacing them. Today, a wide variety of talented writers are actively publishing and transcending traditional genre boundaries.

Art museum attendance is booming. Blockbuster exhibitions travel the world and bring great paintings to increasing numbers of viewers. This is in contrast to but a few decades ago, when most Americans outside of New York had few means of viewing high-quality art. In art publishing, even minor painters have published catalogues full of beautifully reproduced color plates.

Live performance of the arts has flourished as well. From 1965 to 1990, the U.S. went from having 58 symphony orchestras to nearly 300, from 27 opera companies to more than 150, and from 22 nonprofit regional theaters to 500. Contemporary Western culture, especially in the U.S., is thriving.

> *Contemporary Western culture, especially in the U.S., is thriving.*

The market economy continually spurs new artistic innovations. Arguing the worth of particular contemporary creations is more difficult, given the tendencies for disagreement about the present-day culture. (Mozart was controversial in his time, but few dispute his merits today.) Modern creators have offered many deep and lasting works that are universal in their scope and significant in their import, delighting and enriching large numbers of intelligent fans and influencing subsequent artists. We can fully expect many modern and contemporary works to stand the test of time, just as earlier works have, even if we cannot always identify now which are the best.

The most impressive creations of contemporary culture include cinema, rock 'n' roll, Pop Art and Minimalism, modern dance, jazz, genre fiction, and the modern biography, to name but a few. The architectural skylines of Manhattan, Chicago, and Hong Kong were financed and designed almost entirely by the private sector. The exact contents of such a list will vary with taste, but today's culture provides a wide variety of styles, aesthetics, and moods. An individual need not have a very particular set of preferences to love contemporary creations. The 20th century was the age of atonal music and the age of rock star Buddy Holly and film director Steven Spielberg, two life-affirming and celebratory creators.

> *It is no accident that contemporary culture has flourished in today's wealthy society.*

New musical genres continue to blossom. The 20th century saw the development of blues, soul, rhythm and blues, jazz, ragtime, swing, rock, country and western, rap, and bluegrass, as well as more recent forms of electronic music. Some of the most significant modern artists are still around, playing and recording for audiences' enjoyment. Bob Dylan and The Rolling Stones can be heard in concert, still in good form, even if not at their youthful peak.

The Art of the 20th Century

Film became the art of the 20th century, combining drama, music, and high technology to entertain and inspire large audiences. Art movies and independent pictures show continued vitality, but moviegoers around the world want to see mainstream American creations, and for good reasons. Some film buffs complain that "they don't make them like they used to," but the best American efforts of the last 20 years—my personal favorites include "The Thin Blue Line," "Blue Velvet," "The Empire Strikes Back," "Basic Instinct," "Schindler's List," "Dangerous Liaisons," "L.A. Confidential," "Titanic," "Saving Private Ryan," and "The Truman Show"—belie this opinion. This list will not command unanimity, but most viewers will have no trouble noting their own favorites.

New or newly deregulated technologies are likely to induce further cultural innovations. Cable television is expanding rapidly and breaking down the hegemony of the networks. Viewers with satellite dishes are able to choose from hundreds of channels. Cable already offers the world's greatest movies, the modern drama of sporting events, large doses of popular music, and high arts such as ballet, theater, and classical music. Viewers can take a class in Shakespeare without leaving their living rooms, or use foreign dialect channels to learn other languages, thereby enlarging their access to the world's cultural treasures.

Nor is cable the only new artistic medium. The Web, virtual reality technologies, and Hypertext will all revolutionize the delivery of older creations and provide new media for future works.

Finally, quasi-artistic activities are blossoming like never before. Fashion, decoration, cuisine, sports, product design, computer graphics, and commercial art—to name just a few examples—continue to flourish. As recently as 20 years ago, Thai food was not available in most American cities; now, Thai restaurants dot the suburbs as well. Although these fields are not art in the narrow sense, they bring beauty and drama into our lives. A beautifully decorated home or a luxurious shopping mall delight us and appeal to our aesthetic sense. The question "What is art?" has become less fruitful with the growing diversity of capitalist production.

How Markets Support Culture

It is no accident that contemporary culture has flourished in today's wealthy society. Most of the great cultural eras of the past—ancient Athens and Rome, early China, medieval Islamic civilization, the Italian Renaissance, 19th-century Europe, and 20th-century modernism—came in societies that were relatively wealthy and commercial for their time. Nowadays, most of the important works in film, music, literature, painting, and sculpture are sold as commodities. Contemporary art is capitalist art, and the history of art has been a history of the struggle to establish markets.

Creators have the best chance of living from their work in a wealthy, capitalist society. Artists and audiences alike have more leisure time and are freed from tiresome physical labor. The larger size of the market supports a greater diversity of products in artistic and non-artistic realms. Accordingly, the number of individuals who work as full-time creators has risen steadily for centuries.

Capitalism increases the independence of the artist from the immediate demands of the culture-consuming public. The wealth of a market economy funds alternative sources of financial support, such as private foundations, universities, bequests from wealthy relatives, and day jobs. These funding sources allow artists to invest in skills, undertake long-term projects, and control their fate. Ironically, artists who care about art, rather than money, have the best chance in a system based on money and commercial incentives.

Wealthy societies give artists the greatest chance of financial independence and thus creative independence. Beethoven wrote: "I am not out to be a musical usurer as you think, who writes only to become rich, by no means! Yet, I love an independent life, and this I cannot have without a small income." A steady income allows artists to purchase the necessary materials for artistic creation, such as paint and canvas, or, in the case of avantgardist Damien Hirst, sharks and formaldehyde.

> **"** *The pessimists focus on the decline of what they already appreciate and neglect the rise of what is yet to come.* **"**

The painters and sculptors of the Italian Renaissance were businessmen who produced for profit and negotiated hard bargains. Mozart wrote: "Believe me, my sole purpose is to make as much money as possible; for after good health it is the best thing to have." Capitalism allows artists to commercialize their product and sell to large numbers, if they so wish, thereby mobilizing greed in the service of creativity.

Many arts depend on the technological innovations delivered by capitalism. Paper is taken for granted today, but in earlier eras, its high expense significantly limited the output of writers and artists. Photography, cinema, and electronic reproduction of music were not possible until relatively recent times. Advances in medicine allow artists to live to older ages, and birth control permits female creators to manage their careers more effectively.

Why Cultural Pessimism?

Western culture has been on an upswing since at least the year 1000. Innovation and preservation of the past have blossomed. Why then has cultural pessimism had so much influence? Why do a range of critics from Marxists to neo-conservatives attack contemporary culture for its commercialism?

Cognitive biases induce observers to give cultural pessimism more plausibility than it deserves. The pessimists focus on the decline of what they already appreciate and neglect the rise of what is yet to come. It is easy to perceive the loss of what is known and harder to discern forthcoming surprises. Even if long-term trends are positive, culture may appear to be deteriorating.

> *Some kinds of cultural pessimism spring from lack of imagination.*

Observers unfairly compare the entirety of modern culture against the very best of the past. No matter how vital contemporary culture may be, one's favorite novels, movies, and recordings were not all produced just yesterday. Anyone's favorite epochs, including those of the cultural optimist, will lie at some point in the past. Each field, therefore, will appear to have declined, but this is an illusion. Creativity is not necessarily drying up, but, rather, the past contains more accumulated achievement than does any single point in time, such as the present. Given that the world continues to produce creative works, cultural pessimism will appear more and more persuasive. As every year goes by, the past contains an increasing amount of culture, relative to the present.

We consume contemporary culture less efficiently than we consume the culture of the past. Eighteenth-century music critics did not commonly understand that Haydn and Mozart were categorically superior to Christoph Gluck, Luigi Cherubini, Domenico Cimarosa, and Andre Modeste Gretry. Years of debate and listening were needed for the truth to become obvious. Similarly, we are not yet sure who are the truly seminal performers in modern popular music or contemporary art. It takes decades, and sometimes even centuries, to separate the cultural wheat from the chaff.

Most great creators, even those who now strike us as conservative, faced great opposition in their day. The French Impressionists were rejected by the artistic mainstream and considered to be garish and unstructured. Mozart's music was deemed too dissonant by many of his contemporaries. One critic charged Anton Bruckner with being "the greatest living musical peril, a tonal Antichrist . . . [who] composes nothing but high treason, revolution and murder . . . poisoned with the sulphur of Hell."

Older audiences often cannot appreciate new and innovative cultural products. Many people devote their maximum attention to culture in their youth. Between the ages of 15 and 25, for instance, the mind is receptive to new influences; individuals are searching for their identity; and, more often than not, youth are rebelling against their elders. For many, this serves as a formative period for cultural taste. Over time, however, marriage, children, and jobs crowd out the opportunity to discover new products. In their eyes, culture appears to be drying up and declining, creating yet further support for pessimism.

Some individuals hold pessimistic attitudes to support their elitism. Elitists need to feel that they belong to a privileged minority. Contemporary culture, though, is massive in size, diverse in scope, and widely disseminated. Elitists have a hard time sustaining their self-images if they admit that today's culture is wonderful and vibrant. Celebrating the dynamism of modern creations ascribes aesthetic virtues and insights to a very large class of artistic producers and consumers, contra elitism.

The diversity of modern culture implies that much trash will be produced, providing fodder for pessimism and elitism. We should keep these low-quality outputs in proper perspective and view them as a luxury that only diverse and wealthy societies can afford.

Broadening the Imagination

Some kinds of cultural pessimism spring from lack of imagination. We should not look for cultural innovation to recur in the same areas; if anything we should expect the opposite. There is no 20th-century Homer or Aeschylus, but we do have film director Alfred Hitchcock, jazz musician Duke Ellington, and architect Frank Lloyd Wright.

Cultural pessimism has been around as long as culture. Pessimistic attacks have been leveled for centuries, although the target has changed frequently. Many moralists and philosophers, including Plato, criticized theater and poetry for their corrupting influence. Books became a target after the onset of publishing. Eighteenth-century pessimists accused novels of preventing readers from thinking, preaching disobedience to parents (note the contradictory charges), undermining women's sense of subservience, breaking down class distinctions, and making readers sick. Libraries, especially privately run circulating ones, were another target. As author Edward Mangin remarked in 1808: "There is scarcely a street of the metropolis, or a village in the country, in which a circulating library may not be found: nor is there a corner of the empire, where the English language is understood, that has not suffered from the effects of this institution."

In the 18th and 19th centuries, the targets included epistolary romances, newspapers, opera, the music hall, photography, and instrumental virtuosos, such as Franz Liszt and Niccolo Paganini. The 20th century brought the scapegoats of radio, movies, modern art, professional sports, the automobile, television, rhythm and blues, rock 'n' roll, comic books, MTV videos, and rap music. Each new medium or genre has been accused of corrupting youth and promoting excess sensuality, political subversion, and moral relativism.

I, however, am a cultural optimist—one who believes that modern commercial society stimulates artistic creativity and diversity. Capitalist art consists fundamentally of bringing the consumer and producer together. Therein lies its exhilarating, challenging, and poetic nature. Marketplace art is about the meeting of minds and hearts. We should not deplore modern culture, as the pessimists do. Rather we should recognize its fundamentally capitalist nature, which implies creativity, entertainment, innovation, and, above all, diversity.

5

The State of the Family Reveals America's Decline

William J. Bennett

William J. Bennett is an author and social commentator whose books include The Broken Hearth: Reversing the Moral Collapse of the American Family, *from which the following viewpoint is excerpted,* The Book of Virtues: A Treasury of Great Moral Stories, *and* Moral Compass: Stories for a Life's Journey.

Marriage and the family are bedrock institutions in nearly every civilization. Strong family ties confer numerous benefits upon individuals, including a reliable support network, a sense of pride, motivation for admirable conduct, and a framework for acceptable sexual activity. Recently, the sanctity of marriage and family has been threatened by liberalism and the disappearance of decorum in society. The results have been disastrous for American culture: skyrocketing divorce rates, an increase in out-of-wedlock births, more children being raised without fathers, and an unprecedented number of cohabiting couples. To reverse these troubling trends, supporters of the family must join together with people in positions of leadership to aggressively assert their goal to fortify marriage and strengthen the family unit. In addition, more public policies that support the family must be enacted. Determination is necessary to reclaim America's most important cultural institution.

Marriage and family are cultural universals. Everywhere, throughout history, they have been viewed as the standard to which most humans should aspire. This is not happenstance; it is, rather, a natural response to basic human needs— basic to individuals, and basic to society.

A Network of Kinsmen

How do marriage and family answer to basic human and social needs? For one thing, as the anthropologists remind us, the marriage of one man and one woman establishes an intricate network of relatives and "kinsmen"—and, with this, certain built-in expectations, reciprocal obligations, and formal responsibilities. Scholars point to the historical dimension of this vital social function. "They are our enemies, and so we marry them" is how the Zulus[1] express the age-old practice of creating, through marriage, powerful alliances among groups that might otherwise have been strangers or even enemies (in French, the word *alliance* still refers to marriage). Similarly, it has been suggested, the reason behind the universal prohibition of incest may have to do not just with avoiding harmful genetic consequences but with encouraging the domestication, as it were, of disparate and potentially warring lineages.

> *The marriage of one man and one woman establishes an intricate network of relatives and 'kinsmen.'*

For us, today, the "kinsman" aspect of marriage and family operates in different but still clearly related ways. When you marry, people previously unknown to you take on a special place in your life and have certain claims on you, not because of who they are, but because of the title they bear: cousin, daughter-in-law, uncle. That is what it means to be part of a family, a condition whose liabilities have long been the stuff of folklore and countless in-law jokes, but whose benefits are similarly a matter of indisputable record.

[Researcher] David W. Murray, whose work has heavily in-

---

1. The Zulu are a tribe of people centered in the Natal Province of South Africa.

fluenced my thinking on this subject, says that when men and women marry, they acquire, for better and for worse, all the "entangled wiring" of each other's families. A marriage, in other words, is not merely an exchange of vows between two individual people but an extraordinary social moment in which two different families and sets of friends come together in a "relationship of affinity" based on a formal, publicly recognized, legal commitment. This "entanglement," Murray writes, "is stabilizing—not only in the life of the couple and their children, but in the life of the neighborhood."

> **❝ When you marry, you gain an economic and social support system. ❞**

That is one practical benefit: When you marry, you gain an economic and social support system. Relations among friends—even very good friends—tend to be more contingent and less dependable than relations among family members. Friends can easily drop out of your life; relatives are usually there for the duration.

Assume, for example, that you were in desperate need of an organ transplant. Your best friend *might* be willing to donate his kidney to save your life, but such a gesture would be an unexpected and quite extraordinary act of generosity. With family members things are altogether different. There is an inherent "should-ness" to family that is found in no other human arrangement.

Or consider a less dramatic but far more common scenario: A friend who is intelligent, energetic, and ambitious but who, in order to advance professionally, needs to borrow $30,000 to complete his graduate degree. To whom will he more readily and naturally turn? To you, his friend, or, like so many of us, to his in-laws? The answer is obvious. And now suppose this same friend is living with a young woman to whom he is not married. Will he *then* turn to her parents for financial help? The answer, to put it mildly, is far less obvious.

Whether we are talking about medical needs or home loans, college tuition, cash help, child care, health care, emergency shelter, access to transportation, or so much else, marriage and family provide a more extensive and reliable support system than is available to the unmarried. Most of us recognize an obligation, unstated but real, to look after the well-being of those to whom we are related, whether we are fond of them or not. [Poet] Robert Frost once described home as "the place where, when you have to go there, they have to take you in." Family is like that: It creates ties that include, but run much deeper than, personal preference.

Functions of Marriage and Family

Marriage and family perform other functions as well. Families place upon us certain expectations—including, as was once commonly understood, the expectation that we will not bring dishonor upon the family name. To put it positively, the fact that we represent not only ourselves but our families can be a source of authentic pride, and authentic pride (as opposed to false pride) is a powerful motivator of right conduct.

Marriage and family help establish rules for sexual conduct. Throughout all time, societies have known that sex is not only the most powerful of human passions but an activity whose repercussions can be hugely destructive, wrecking human lives and inflicting wounds that can easily last a lifetime. That is why all societies have undertaken to guide sexuality by means of ritual and law.

> *Marriage and family help establish rules for sexual conduct.*

Marriage establishes a sexual framework that is at once restrictive and liberating. At once, it enables and it sets boundaries. In [researcher] George Gilder's pithy words, "Under a regime of monogamy there are limits. One may covet one's neighbor's wife . . . but one generally leaves it at that." But under this selfsame "regime," a married couple can be both intimate and open, freed from the intense competition that is an intrinsic element of male-female relations. In marriage, our sexual needs are directed toward emotionally and morally constructive ends.

But the chief argument in the anthropological case for marriage has to do with, precisely, those ends: that is, with procreation, children, the next generation. In the matter-of-fact phrase of one highly regarded manual of ethnography, "Marriage is a union between a man and a woman such that the children born to the woman are recognized as legitimate offspring of both partners." If, as has been said, children are the ultimate "illegal aliens," then the purpose of marriage is to provide them with the full rights of human citizenship, including public legitimacy, social identity, legal recognition, a lineage, a cultural tradition, and an estate.

When it comes to the nurture and protection of children, moreover, marriage is by far the best arrangement ever devised—which is one reason we find it in all human societies, primitive and modern, ancient and contemporary, Western and non-Western. Cultures that differ on many things all agree that children should not be born outside of marriage, an institution that lays the legal foundation for the family that will be formed by it.

> **"** *Cultures that differ on many things all agree that children should not be born outside of marriage.* **"**

In imposing obligations on parents with regard to children, marriage ensures that every child has a *pater*, the socially recognized father who assumes full responsibility for that child, and not merely a *genitor*, a biological father. It also establishes the cultural context in which children learn to respect the authority of parents. When a child is born to a marriage, mother, father, and all their relatives are now attached to that creature whose well-being has been placed within their care. Later, much later, when the children grow up and the parents grow old, the situation subtly reverses itself; the web of obligation remains constant and unbroken.

The Broken Web

But I have been speaking too abstractly and, alas, too positively. Can we say of American society at large that in it, for the most part, the web of obligation remains constant and unbroken? Hardly; otherwise, we would not be hearing so much, including from the likes of me, about the crisis of marriage and the family, or about the powerlessness of government alone to affect that crisis.

My argument here is that the family is and always has been the first and most important incubator of those habits of trust, altruism, responsibility, and mutual obligation on which civil society depends—in [researcher] Michael Novak's words, the first, best, and original department of health, education, and welfare. Any society desirous of preserving itself has, therefore, the strongest possible interest in the well-being of its families, and especially in the safety and protection of its children. That interest, it is fair to say, has been subverted by the steady assault on marriage and family . . . a process colluded in by government, furthered by the hedonistic and liberationist march of our culture, and abetted by the erosion of once inviolate boundaries of decorum—whether in the White House or on the movie screen, in our neighborhoods or, sad to say, even in some of our churches. . . .

Since 1960, the divorce rate has more than doubled, out-of-wedlock births have skyrocketed from one in twenty to one in three, the percentage of single-parent families has more than tripled, the number of couples cohabiting has increased more than elevenfold, the fertility rate has decreased by almost half. In record numbers, we have seen fathers deserting their wives and children—and being permitted to do so without reproach or penalty of any kind. We have seen stay-at-home mothers mocked. We have seen the advent of something called the "parenting deficit"—a polite way of saying that many parents are, in effect, absent from their children's lives.

> **Once almost universally regarded as a sacred covenant, marriage and family life now strike many people as provisional undertakings.**

Along with this transformation of reality, we have also seen a dramatic shift in people's *attitudes* toward marriage and the family: toward the expectations that should govern male-female relationships, toward the responsibilities of parenthood, and toward sex itself, which has been untethered from any notion of committed love. Once almost universally regarded as a sacred covenant, marriage and family life now strike many people as provisional undertakings at best. They have been encouraged in this mental direction by feminists, academic analysts with an agenda, and libertines masquerading as liberationists: a de facto coalition of cultural voices arguing that the very institution of the family is inherently oppressive, a reflection of the power preferences of males, or at best an arbitrary construct infinitely adaptable to whatever ends free individuals may wish to devise for it.

> *We are not helpless or without recourse when it comes to repairing damage we have sustained.*

Applied to the laws, the morals, and the civic and religious life of our society, these notions and others like them have wrought carnage. Indeed, when we think back on the recent past, does it not begin to seem naive in the extreme that we should ever have expected otherwise? There are traditional moral understandings that may be refined and qualified, but that cannot be flouted with impunity. There is a natural order that we may build on and improve but that we attempt to do away with at peril of the very fabric of our lives, our happiness, our true and solid contentment. Too many of us have attempted to do just that and have reaped a whirlwind.

Guidelines for Restoration

What, then, should we do? Have we reached the condition, so well described by the Roman historian Livy, where we can neither endure our vices nor face their remedy, unwilling perhaps to go on indefinitely with a society whose families are so fragmented but unable to do what is required to strengthen them? In pointing a way out of our predicament, I wish to offer not so much a detailed blueprint as a few essential guidelines.

The first order of business must be to develop a new and clearer frame of mind. Sadly, there are those who have concluded from surveying the damage that the collapse of the family is indeed irreversible. (I exclude those who have consciously worked for the collapse of the family, and welcome it.) My response is that this need not be so, and that we must not allow it to be so.

Other social problems once thought to be intractable have, after all, yielded to resolute action, and in some cases with stunning swiftness. During the second half of the 1990s, welfare rolls decreased by almost half, and the murder rate dropped to its lowest level since the 1960s. And we have made progress on other "entrenched" social problems as well: racism, poverty, the use of illegal drugs, drunk driving. Even some of the pathologies related to the American family have slowed or diminished in recent years. We are not helpless or without recourse when it comes to repairing damage we have sustained. Our injuries are in most cases self-inflicted; they can be self-corrected. They are the consequences of moral choice; they can be redressed by means of other, better choices.

> *At every level of government we need to implement* policies *that strengthen both marriage and the family.*

Second, we need to be realistic. Many of the changes, especially the economic and technological changes, that have affected our families will not be undone. Many, indeed, should not be undone. Over the centuries . . . quite a few aspects of marriage and family life have changed for the better. To take some obvious examples: Unlike in ages past, the vast majority of us do not practice or believe in arranged marriages, let alone in polygamy, nor do we countenance for a moment the denial of a woman's legal rights in marriage. In deciding to marry, we moderns place the emphasis on voluntary and reciprocal affection, on emotional fulfillment, friendship, and companionship. The last few decades, moreover, have seen other changes in marriage and family life. Many men are more involved in the early raising of their children, and wives in truly bad marriages have more avenues for protecting themselves or, if necessary, for escape.

Surely this is to the good and constitutes authentic progress. If we insist on retaining an [idyllic] image of family life . . . we will certainly fail in our efforts. And yet many Americans who have no desire to regress into a lost past are nevertheless appalled at the social chaos we have created and are eager for what might be called a *restoration*, or what the writer Tom Wolfe has called a "great relearning."

The moment is ripe. The Promethean arrogance of the last decades, having wrought so much misery, has shown signs of slowly exhausting itself, which means the ground may be readier for fresh starts than it once was even a short while ago. My hope is that many more of us will join in recognizing the opportunity and in building on it.

Third, and in line with what I have just said, we need to disseminate the facts—the truth—about marriage and family life, for facts are our greatest allies. The more we know and can tell about the real-life benefits of marriage and family—and the more we know and can tell about the real-life harm of the effort to undo them—the stronger becomes our case.

Fourth, Americans in positions of leadership need to assert and to argue—publicly, consistently, and compellingly—that their goal is to fortify marriage and the family. This message can come from figures in many different fields: religion, education, entertainment, sports, business, medicine, law, the military, politics. To take an obvious example, President George W. Bush could find few more significant uses of his bully pulpit than in helping to shape public attitudes toward the family for the better.

Fifth, at every level of government we need to implement *policies* that strengthen both marriage and the family. I have already proposed a number of such policies, from reforming no-fault divorce laws to supporting the Defense of Marriage Act to cutting off future welfare benefits to unmarried teen mothers. More can be found in a document titled *The Marriage Movement: A Statement of Principles*. Enacting these reforms would mark a positive advance if only because for far too many years our government and our laws have put themselves on the side of decomposition, not on the side of restoration. But laws also give expression to our moral beliefs. The civil rights legislation of the 1950s and 1960s represented a sterling example of statecraft as soulcraft. It is time we undertook to fight with equal ardor and determination on behalf of our most precious institution.

6

A Renewed Commitment to Marriage Could Reverse the Decline of American Culture

David Blankenhorn

David Blankenhorn is president of the New York–based Institute for American Values. Before founding the institute, he worked for seven years for several nonprofit policy and advocacy organizations in Virginia and Massachusetts. He graduated from Harvard University and received an MA in history from Warwick University in England. He is the author of Fatherless America, *and his articles on family and civic issues have appeared in many publications.*

The social institution of marriage has become considerably weaker since the 1960s. This decline of marriage resulted from an increase in out-of-wedlock births and skyrocketing divorce rates. As a result, fewer children are raised in homes with two biological parents, the population level has stagnated, and restraints on adult sexual behavior have been loosened. In the 1990s a grassroots "marriage movement" gained momentum and has encouraged social activists and legislators to revive cultural support for marriage. More organizations adopted a pro-marriage position and many states passed legislation that support marriage. Consequently, increases in the num-

David Blankenhorn, "The Marriage Problem," *American Experiment Quarterly,* Spring 2003. Copyright © 2003 by the Center of the American Experiment. Reproduced by permission.

ber of children living in two-parent homes have been seen. Despite these minor successes, the marriage movement has a long way to go before the effects of a divorced culture are thoroughly mitigated. Intense effort on behalf of marriage supporters is necessary to achieve these goals.

O ver the course of three decades, from the mid-1960s through at least the mid-1990s, marriage as a social institution got steadily and dramatically weaker.

During these years, American adults became significantly less likely to get married and stay married. The annual number of marriages per 1,000 unmarried women dropped substantially, as did the proportion of all American adults who were married. And if they were married, they were less likely to describe their marriage as "very happy" [according to researchers David Popenoe amd Barbara Dafoe Whitehead].

> **//** *Scholars and other leaders view the weakening of marriage as a genuine societal crisis.* **//**

During this period, very high rates of divorce and steadily increasing rates of unwed childbearing produced a steady decline of the married-couple, mother-father child-raising family, and a steadily decreasing proportion of American children under the age of eighteen living with their two biological, married parents.

Over these approximately three decades, according to many measurements, married-couple families became less able to carry out their basic social functions of:

• Maintaining the population level. The total fertility rate for American married couples is about 1.6. That's below the replacement level and about half of what it was in the late 1950s.

• Regulating adult sexual behavior.

• Socializing children and in other ways caring for family members.

During this period, familism as a societal value increasingly lost ground to other, and in some cases competing, social values, such as individualism and consumerism.

This story line of the roughly thirty-year decline of marriage is well known among experts and in the society as a whole. Its basic dimensions are not in dispute.

Neither are the basic social consequences of this trend any longer in dispute. Increasingly, scholars and other leaders view the weakening of marriage as a genuine societal crisis. The respected scholar James Q. Wilson recently described the weakening of marriage as "the most important domestic problem in the country." It drives or sustains a diversity of social problems such as child poverty, weapons-related violence, educational failure, teen suicide, child and adolescent mental health problems, teen pregnancy, and many others.

Here's one example: one of every three divorces in the United States resulting in the physical separation of a father from his children plunges the mother and children into poverty. Father absence due to marital failure is a primary cause of child poverty in the United States.

These trends, while probably most advanced in the United States and in the other English-speaking countries, are to some degree global in nature, leading some scholars to speculate about a "world trend" toward the "postnuclear family"—societies in which the married-couple, mother-father child-raising unit is no longer normative for the society as a whole, but instead is viewed merely as one of many ethically and socially acceptable personal life style options.

The Marriage Movement

In the 1990s, first a grassroots fatherhood movement, and then a marriage movement, emerged in the United States seeking to improve child well-being by strengthening fatherhood, improving the quality and stability of marriage as a social institution, and reducing unwed childbearing and unnecessary divorce. As a result, since the early 1990s, impressive progress has been made in changing U.S. elite and public opinion, as well as in stimulating political and grassroots action, on the social importance of marriage.

How much progress? "On the heels of a fatherhood movement," [researcher] Alex Kotlowitz recently wrote in the *New York Times*, more and more young couples in inner cities "are considering marriage." Kotlowitz's Frontline television documentary, *Let's Get Married*, which aired in November 2002 on PBS, focuses on what the documentary calls the "burgeoning marriage movement." At least at the level of the public debate, there has been much recent progress in making the case for marriage and in putting the marriage problem on the national agenda. As Kotlowitz reports: "Now, everyone from the government to intellectuals are pushing marriage."

How much progress have we made? As the syndicated columnist Jane Eisner recently put it, there is a "growing consensus" that the question of renewing marriage—*How do we strengthen marriage as the primary social institution to rear children?*—is now "the central question of American life."

> *❝Now, everyone from the government to intellectuals are pushing marriage.❞*

Reflecting on the year 2002, she continues: "Liberals, in particular, heard the wake-up call this year. No longer confined to the outer reaches of the Religious Right, the 'marriage movement' is moving center stage, as those on the political left are belatedly adding their voices to this necessary debate."

In *The Nation*, Judith Stacey, a strong critic of the marriage movement, recently complained angrily "the marriage movement is busting out all over, a harbinger of 'faith-based' approaches to social reform." The *Observer* of London reported "the pro-marriage movement is gaining strength on both sides of the Atlantic." [In August 2002], the *Orange County Register* reported on the "growing marriage movement meant to slow the divorce rate."

In the elite media, an important intellectual and political corner was turned in mid-2001, when the *New York Times*, after years of journalistic equivocation and entrenched skepticism, finally reported in a front-page story that:

> . . . a powerful consensus has emerged in recent years among social scientists, as well as state and federal policy makers. It sees single-parent families as the dismal foundries that produced decades of child poverty, delinquency, and crime. And it views the rise of such families, which began in the early 1960s and continued until about five years ago, as a singularly important indicator of child pathology.

And:

> From a child's point of view, according to a growing body of social research, the most supportive house-

hold is one with two biological parents in a low-conflict marriage.

Not only newly marriage-friendly sensibilities in the media and elsewhere, but also new pro-marriage public and private sector policy initiatives, are beginning to emerge.

In the early 1990s, for example, few scholars, and even fewer academic professional associations, dared even to address the topic of marriage, much less suggest that marriage might be a beneficial institution worthy of societal support. In fact, two of the most relevant professional associations, the National Council on Family Relations and the American Association of Marriage and Family Therapy, consistently refused to address this subject. (Yes, it's actually true that an organization with the word marriage in its name had by the mid-1990s long since abandoned any commitment to, or even interest in, marriage.) That refusal led Diane Sollee, a marriage therapist and a member of both organizations, to start a new group, the Coalition for Marriage, Family, and Couples Education, now popularly called Smart Marriages. In 1997, Sollee's first Smart Marriages conference drew 400 participants. The 2002 Smart Marriages conference drew about 1,700 participants.

Interestingly, responding to the success of Sollee's organization and other recent marriage initiatives, even the older organizations are slowly beginning to re-engage the issue.

> *The trend of family fragmentation . . . largely stopped in its tracks in about 1995.*

The 2002 annual meeting of the mostly academic National Council on Family Relations featured a debate on the question, "Is Strengthening Marriage to Reduce the Divorce Rate a Workable Strategy for Policy and Intervention?" The announced theme of this group's 2003 annual meeting is, "What is the Future of Marriage?" These topics would have been unimaginable for this group even five years ago.

In 1990, the number of grassroots efforts aiming to strengthen marriage was extremely small. Today, there are hundreds of such efforts, including broad, well-structured, community-based efforts in Grand Rapids, Michigan; Chattanooga, Tennessee; and Cleveland, Ohio, and a regional effort called Families Northwest based in Seattle, Washington. Marriage Savers, a recently founded ministry devoted to strengthening marriage, now has multi-denominational, church-based "community marriage policies" in about 150 communities in thirty-five states.

> **❝** *If [recent changes] continue, they will change the lives of millions of American children and families for the better.* **❞**

The Institute for American Values' work in this area has also helped to shape public arguments, conduct and disseminate scholarly research, incubate key books and articles, convene leaders, and launch initiatives that have contributed to building the marriage movement.

Government policy makers have also become more interested in this issue. Since the late 1990s, several states—Florida, Oklahoma, Utah, Louisiana, Minnesota, Maryland, Tennessee, Arkansas, and Arizona—have passed laws or initiated programs aimed at strengthening marriage.

At the level of federal policy, many analysts believe that the welfare reforms of 1996 have led to modest but measurable positive influences on trends in marriage and family formation among low-income Americans. In addition, a leader of the marriage movement, Wade Horn, was appointed by President Bush in 2000 to serve as assistant secretary for Families and Children at the U.S. Department of Health and Human Services. Horn, who was president of the National Fatherhood Initiative, has been the point-person and a leader within the administration in developing and proposing legislation intended to continue and enhance efforts at marriage education and family formation as a part of welfare re-authorization. He also has initiated several funding, research, and public education efforts within HHS aimed at promoting marriage.

Finally, consider some encouraging (if tentative) demographic news. A series of recent independent reports, based largely on data from the 2000 Census, suggest that the trend of family fragmentation, which many analysts had assumed to be unstoppable, largely stopped in its tracks in about 1995. Up until then, yearly increases in unwed childbearing and divorce had resulted in ever-greater proportions of children living in one-parent homes.

The proportion of all American families with children under eighteen that were headed by married couples reached an all-time low in the mid-1990s—about 72.9 percent in 1996 and 72.4 percent in 1997. But since then the number has stabilized. The figure for 2000 was 73 percent. Similarly, the proportion of all American children living in two-parent homes reached an all-time low in the mid-1990s, and has since stabilized. In fact, the proportion of children in two-parent homes increased from 68 percent in 1999 to 69.1 percent in 2000.

> // *Amazingly, the 'm-word' is almost mainstream these days in policy, academic, and media circles.* //

Looking only at white, non-Hispanic children, a study by [researchers] Allan Dupree and Wendell Primus found that the proportion of these children living with two married parents stopped its downward descent during the late 1990s, and even increased slightly from 1999 to 2000, rising from 77.3 to 78.2 percent. Another study from the Urban Institute found that, among all American children, the proportion living with their two biological or adoptive parents increased by 1.2 percent from 1997 to 1999. During the same period the proportion of children living in stepfamilies (or blended families) decreased by 0.1 percent and the proportion living in single-parent homes decreased by 2 percent. (The study found that in 1999 about 64 percent of all American children lived with their two biological or adoptive parents, while about 25 percent lived with one parent and about 8 percent lived in a blended or stepfamily.) Among low-income children, the decline in the proportion living in single-parent homes was even more pronounced, dropping from 44 percent in 1997 to 41 percent in 1999.

Here is perhaps the most promising statistic. From 1995 to 2000, the proportion of African American children living in two-parent, married-couple homes rose from 34.8 to 38.9 percent, a significant increase in just five years, representing the clear cessation and even reversal of the long-term shift toward black family fragmentation.

These changes are not large or definitive. But they are certainly suggestive. And if they continue, they will change the lives of millions of American children and families for the better.

What can be done to nurture and accelerate this progress? What new strategies and arguments can be deployed by fatherhood and marriage leaders to turn these hopeful developments and glimmers of good news into a sustained marriage renewal, leading to more children growing up in stable, two-parent homes? In short, what's next for the marriage movement? . . .

An Intellectual Strategic Plan

What should be our movement's primary intellectual goals for the coming months? Considering the movement as a whole, let me suggest these major intellectual goals. . . .

1. To convene influential marriage scholars and leaders to commission and discuss papers, deliberate, and produce a joint statement describing the status and proposing the future direction of the marriage movement, including its major social and policy objectives for the coming decade.
2. To collect and disseminate credible data showing which marriage programs are succeeding in strengthening marriage and reducing divorce and unwed childbearing.
3. To draft and urge passage of a U.S. congressional resolution on the benefits and importance of healthy marriages.
4. To respond intellectually to the new critics of "the case for marriage," whose emerging argument appears to be that, while happy marriages are beneficial, troubled or unhappy marriages are not, especially for women. This argument seeks to revive the long influential but recently discredited [researcher] Jesse Bernard thesis of "his marriage/her marriage." It also seeks to shift from a sociological and anthropological discussion of marriage as an institution to a therapeutic discussion of individual (good and bad) marriages, which ignores and indirectly undermines the possibility of evaluating a collective interest in marriage. This naturally leads to evaluating society's legal and other interests in marriage.
5. To change scholarly and public understanding of the consequence of divorce for children by building on Judith Wallerstein's insight that the effects are best mea-

sured not by examining "symptom lists," but instead
by looking at the inner lives—emotional, moral, spiritual—of the children of divorce, particularly as those
children enter young adulthood.

6. To document the continuing shift in the academic
treatment of marriage by quantifying the main trends
in U.S. academic research and scholarly writing on marriage since 1977.

7. To collect and publish information on recent U.S.
trends in marriage and family formation, especially regarding the proportion of U.S. children living with
their two biological, married parents. This information
will largely be drawn from census data.

8. To seek improvements in how the U.S. Census Bureau
and the National Center for Health Statistics collect and
publish data regarding the state of marriage.

9. To evaluate and report on recent scholarship on marriage among African Americans, paying particular attention to evaluating critically those studies suggesting
that marriage is less beneficial to African Americans
than to others.

10. To measure and report the economic consequences of
divorce, including both private and public-sector costs
and transfers, at both state-by-state and national levels.

11. To jump-start a focus on marriage law reform by examining and critiquing currently influential family law
scholarship and proposing alternative directions: examining empirically the relationship between state-level divorce laws and marriage and divorce rates; considering a
range of possible state-level divorce law reforms; and
making recommendations for pro-marriage legal reforms to state policy makers and marriage leaders.

Achieving these goals will be difficult, but we can do it. In
only a few years, the marriage movement has made much
progress. We helped to put an important issue on the national
agenda. Amazingly, the "m-word" is almost mainstream these
days in policy, academic, and media circles. Ten years ago, who
would have predicted it? More importantly, we have been a part
of bringing to a virtual standstill, at least for now, the most
harmful demographic trend of our generation. Again, who
would have predicted it? Not a bad start. Now it's time to really
get going.

7

Dysfunctional Marriages Contribute to America's Decline

E. Mavis Hetherington

E. Mavis Hetherington is a professor of psychology at the University of Virginia. She is the former president of the developmental psychology division of the American Psychological Association and of the Society of Research in Childhood Development in Adolescence. She is well known for her work on the effects of divorced, single-parent families, and remarriage on children's development.

Many social commentators argue that children perform best when raised in a home with married parents than when brought up by a single parent. However, unhappy, abusive, or unsupportive marriages are often more destructive to a child's well-being than divorce. In fact, many children and adults, according to one study, perform better at school and at work once a dysfunctional marriage is dissolved. Public policies aimed at promoting marriage and discouraging divorce often fail to take these factors into account. Policy makers must acknowledge that preserving a marriage at all costs is not always the best solution to family problems and that children of divorce do not always exhibit problems later in life.

On average, recent studies show parents and children in married families are happier, healthier, wealthier, and better adjusted than those in single-parent households. But these averages conceal wide variations. Before betting the farm on marriage—with a host of new government programs aimed at promoting traditional two-parent families and discouraging divorce—policy makers should take another look at the research. It reveals that there are many kinds of marriage and not all are salutary. Nor are all divorces and single-parent experiences associated with lasting distress. It is not the inevitability of positive or negative responses to marriage or divorce that is striking, but the diversity of them.

Men do seem to benefit simply from the state of being married. Married men enjoy better health and longevity and fewer psychological and behavioral problems than single men. But women, studies repeatedly have found, are more sensitive to the emotional quality of the marriage. They benefit from being in a well-functioning marriage, but in troubled marriages they are likely to experience depression, immune-system breakdowns, and other health-related problems.

We saw the same thing in the project I directed at the Hetherington Laboratory at the University of Virginia, which followed 1,400 divorced families, including 2,500 kids, over time, some for as long as 30 years, interviewing them, testing them, and observing them at home, at school, and in the community. This was the most comprehensive study of divorce and remarriage ever undertaken; for policy makers, the complexity of the findings is perhaps its most important revelation.

Good Marriages, Bad Marriages

By statistical analysis, we identified five broad types of marriage—ranging from "pursuer-distancer" marriages, which we found were the most likely to end in divorce, to disengaged marriages, to operatic marriages, and finally to "cohesive-individuated" marriages and traditional marriages, which had the least risk of instability.

To describe them briefly:

• Pursuer-distancer marriages are those mismatches in which one spouse, usually the wife, wants to confront and discuss problems and feelings and the other, usually the husband, wants to avoid confrontations and either denies problems or withdraws.

• In disengaged marriages, couples share few interests, activities, or friends. Conflict is low, but so is affection and sexual satisfaction.

• Operatic marriages involve couples who like to function

at a level of extreme emotional arousal. They are intensely attracted, attached, and volatile, given both to frequent fighting and to passionate lovemaking.

• Cohesive-individuated marriages are the yuppie and feminist ideal, characterized by equity, respect, warmth, and mutual support, but also by both partners retaining the autonomy to pursue their own goals and to have their own friends.

• Traditional marriages are those in which the husband is the main income producer and the wife's role is one of nurturance, support, and home and child care. These marriages work well as long as both partners continue to share a traditional view of gender roles.

We found that not just the risk of divorce, but also the extent of women's psychological and health troubles, varies according to marriage type—with wives in pursuer-distancer and disengaged marriages experiencing the most problems, those in operatic marriages significantly fewer, and those in cohesive-individuated and traditional marriages the fewest. Like so many other studies, we found that men's responses are less nuanced; the only differentiation among them was that men in pursuer-distancer marriages have more problems than those in the other four types.

The issue is not simply the amount of disagreement in the marriage; disagreements, after all, are endemic in close personal relations. It is *how* people disagree and solve problems— how they interact that turns out to be closely associated with both the duration of their marriages and the well-being of wives and, to a lesser extent, husbands. Contempt, hostile criticism, belligerence, denial, and withdrawal erode a marriage. Affection, respect, trust, support, and making the partner feel valued and worthwhile strengthen the relationship.

Good Divorces, Bad Divorces

Divorce experiences also are varied. Initially, especially in marriages involving children, divorce is miserable for most couples. In the early years, ex-spouses typically must cope with lingering attachments; with resentment and anger, self-doubts, guilt, depression, and loneliness; with the stress of separation from children or of raising them alone; and with the loss of social networks and, for women, of economic security. Nonetheless, we found that a gradual recovery usually begins by the end of the second year. And by six years after divorce, 80 percent of both men and women have moved on to build reasonably or exceptionally fulfilling lives.

Indeed, about 20 percent of the women we observed eventually emerged from divorce enhanced and exhibiting competencies they never would have developed in an unhappy or constraining marriage. They had gone back to school or work to ensure the economic stability of their families, they had built new social networks, and they had become involved and effective parents and socially responsible citizens. Often they had happy second marriages. Divorce had offered them an opportunity to build new and more satisfying relationships and the freedom they needed for personal growth. This was especially true for women moving from a pursuer-distancer or disengaged marriage, or from one in which a contemptuous or belligerent husband undermined their self-esteem and child-rearing practices. Divorced men, we found, are less likely to undergo such remarkable personal growth; still, the vast majority of the men in our study did construct reasonably happy new lives for themselves.

As those pressing for government programs to promote marriage will no doubt note, we found that the single most important predictor of a divorced parent's subsequent adjustment is whether he or she has formed a new and mutually supportive intimate relationship. But what should also be noticed is that successful re-partnering takes many forms. We found that about 75 percent of men and 60 percent of women eventually remarry, but an increasing number of adults are opting to cohabit instead—or to remain single and meet their need for intimacy with a dating arrangement, a friendship, or a network of friends or family.

> **❝** *[Not] all divorces and single-parent experiences [are] associated with lasting distress.* **❞**

There is general agreement among researchers that parents' re-partnering does not do as much for their children. Both young children and adolescents in divorced and remarried families have been found to have, on average, more social, emotional, academic, and behavioral problems than kids in two-parent, non-divorced families. My own research, and that of many other investigators, finds twice as many serious psychological disorders and behavioral problems—such as teenage pregnancy, dropping out of school, substance abuse, unemployment, and marital breakups—among the offspring of divorced parents as among the children of non-divorced families. This is a closer association than between smoking and cancer.

However, the troubled youngsters remain a relatively small proportion of the total. In our study, we found that 75 percent to 80 percent of children and adolescents from divorced families, after a period of initial disruption, are able to cope with the divorce and their new life situation and develop into reasonably or exceptionally well-adjusted individuals. In fact, as we saw with women, some girls eventually emerge from their parents' divorces remarkably competent and responsible. From the divorce experience they also learn how to handle later stresses in their lives.

> *About 20 percent of the women we observed eventually emerged from divorce enhanced and exhibiting competencies they never would have developed in an unhappy or constraining marriage.*

Without ignoring the serious pain and distress experienced by many divorced parents and children, it is important to underscore that substantial research findings confirm the ability of the vast majority to move on successfully.

It is also important to recognize that many of the adjustment problems in parents and children—and much of the inept parenting and destructive family relations, which policy makers have attributed to divorce—actually are present *before* divorce. Being in a dysfunctional family has taken its toll before the breakup occurs.

Predicting the aftermath of divorce is complex, and the truth is obscured if one looks only at averages. Differences in experience or personality account for more variation than the averages would suggest. A number of studies have found, for instance, that adults and children who perceived their pre-divorce life as happy and satisfying tend to be more upset by a marital breakup than those who viewed the marriage as contentious, threatening, or unfulfilling. Other studies show that adults and children who are mature, stable, self-regulated, and adaptable are more likely able to cope with the challenges of divorce. Those who are neurotic, antisocial, and impulsive—and who lack a sense of their own efficacy—are likely to have these characteristics exacerbated by the breakup. In other words, the psychologically poor get poorer after a divorce while the rich often get richer.

The diversity of American marriages makes it unlikely that any one-size-fits-all policy to promote marriage and prevent divorce will be beneficial. Policy makers are now talking about offering people very brief, untested education and counseling programs, but such approaches rarely have long-lasting effects. And they are generally least successful with the very groups that policy makers are most eager to marry off—single mothers and the poor.

In their recent definitive review of the research on family interventions, Phil Cowan, Douglas Powell, and Carolyn Pape Cowan find that the most effective approaches are the most comprehensive ones—those that deal with both parents and children, with family dynamics, and with a family's needs for jobs, education, day care, and/or health care. Beyond that, which interventions work best seems to vary, depending on people's stage of life, the kind of family or ethnic group they are in, and the specific challenges before them.

Strengthening and promoting positive family relationships and improving the many settings in which children develop is a laudable goal. However, policies that constrain or encourage people to remain in destructive marriages—or that push uncommitted couples to marry—are likely to do more harm than good. The same is true of marriage incentives and rewards designed to create traditional families with the husband as the economic provider and the wife as homemaker. If our social policies do not recognize the diversity and varied needs of American families, we easily could end up undermining them.

8

Immigration Strengthens American Culture

Ben Wattenberg

Ben Wattenberg is a senior fellow at the American Enterprise Institute, a conservative research institute. He is also the author of The Birth Dearth *and* Survival 101.

Some Americans fear that allowing many immigrants to come to the United States threatens the American culture. On the contrary, immigration is what keeps the country vital and competitive. Since the birthrate in the United States is decreasing, the population will begin to shrink without immigrants. Furthermore, immigrants are the best spokespeople for democracy and other Western values. They tell their friends and families in their home countries about the many positive aspects of life in America and spread the belief in open government and personal liberty. The United States must continue to accept immigrants in order to strengthen American power and influence around the world.

M any leading thinkers tell us we are now in a culture clash that will determine the course of history, that today's war is for Western civilization itself. There is a demographic dimension to this "clash of civilizations." While certain of today's demographic signals bode well for America, some look very bad. If we are to assess America's future prospects, we must start by asking: "Who are we?," "Who will we be?," and "How will we relate

Ben Wattenberg, "Immigration: A Cause of the Clash of Civilizations . . . or a Solution to It?" *The American Enterprise*, vol. 13, March 2002, pp. 22–24. Copyright © 2002 by *The American Enterprise*, a Magazine of Politics, Business, and Culture. Reproduced by permission.

to the rest of the world?" The answers all involve immigration.

As data from the 2000 census trickled out, one item hit the headline jackpot. By the year 2050, we were told, America would be "majority non-white." The census count showed more Hispanics in America than had been expected, making them "America's largest minority." When blacks, Asians, and Native Americans are added to the Hispanic total, the "non-white" population emerges as a large minority, on the way to becoming a small majority around the middle of the twenty-first century.

The first thing worth noting is that these rigid racial definitions are absurd. The whole concept of race as a biological category is becoming ever-more dubious in America. Consider:

Under the Bill Clinton administration's census rules, any American who checks both the black and white boxes on the form inquiring about "race" is counted as black, even if his heritage is, say, one eighth black and seven eighths white. In effect, this enshrines the infamous segregationist view that one drop of black blood makes a person black.

> *What if instead of swamping us, immigration helps us become a stronger nation and a swamper of others in the global competition of civilizations?*

Although most Americans of Hispanic heritage declare themselves "white," they are often inferentially counted as non-white, as in the erroneous *New York Times* headline which recently declared: "Census Confirms Whites Now a Minority" in California.

If those of Hispanic descent, hailing originally from about 40 nations, are counted as a minority, why aren't those of Eastern European descent, coming from about 10 nations, also counted as a minority? (In which case the Eastern European "minority" would be larger than the Hispanic minority.)

But within this jumble of numbers there lies a central truth: America is becoming a universal nation, with significant representation of nearly all human hues, creeds, ethnicities, and national ancestries. Continued moderate immigration will make us an even more universal nation as time goes on. And this process may well play a serious role in determining the outcome of the contest of civilizations taking place across the globe.

And current immigration rates are moderate, even though America admitted more legal immigrants from 1991 to 2000 than in any previous decade—between 10 and 11 million. The highest previous decade was 1901–1910, when 8.8 million people arrived. In addition, each decade now, several million illegal immigrants enter the U.S., thanks partly to ease of transportation.

Immigrants Will Not "Swamp" America

Critics like [political leader] Pat Buchanan say that absorbing all those immigrants will "swamp" the American culture and bring Third World chaos inside our borders. I disagree. Keep in mind: Those 8.8 million immigrants who arrived in the U.S. between 1901 and 1910 increased the total American population by 1 percent per year. (Our numbers grew from 76 million to 92 million during that decade.) In our most recent decade, on the other hand, the 10 million legal immigrants represented annual growth of only 0.36 percent (as the U.S. went from 249 million to 281 million).

Overall, nearly 15 percent of Americans were foreign-born in 1910. In 1999, our foreign-born were about 10 percent of our total. (In 1970, the foreign-born portion of our population was down to about 5 percent. Most of the rebound resulted from a more liberal immigration law enacted in 1965.) Or look at the "foreign stock" data. These figures combine Americans born in foreign lands and their offspring, even if those children have only one foreign-born parent. Today, America's "foreign stock" amounts to 21 percent of the population and heading up. But in 1910, the comparable figure was 34 percent—one third of the entire country—and the heavens did not collapse.

Immigrants to America always have [acculturated].

We can take in more immigrants, if we want to. Should we?
Return to the idea that immigrants could swamp American culture. If that is true, we clearly should not increase our in-

take. But what if instead of swamping us, immigration helps us become a stronger nation and a swamper of others in the global competition of civilizations?

Immigration Keeps America Growing

Immigration is now what keeps America growing. According to the U.N., the typical American woman today bears an average of 1.93 children over the course of her childbearing years. That is mildly below the 2.1 "replacement" rate required to keep a population stable over time, absent immigration. The "medium variant" of the most recent Census Bureau projections posits that the U.S. population will grow from 281 million in 2000 to 397 million in 2050 with expected immigration, but only to 328 million should we choose a path of zero immigration. That is a difference of a population growth of 47 million versus 116 million. (The 47 million rise is due mostly to demographic momentum from previous higher birthrates.) If we have zero immigration with today's low birthrates indefinitely, the American population would eventually begin to shrink, albeit slowly.

> *If America doesn't continue to take in immigrants, it won't continue to grow in the long run.*

Is more population good for America? When it comes to potential global power and influence, numbers can matter a great deal. Taxpayers, many of them, pay for a fleet of aircraft carriers. And on the economic side it is better to have a customer boom than a customer bust. (It may well be that Japan's stagnant demography is one cause of its decade-long slump.) The environmental case could be debated all day long, but remember that an immigrant does not add to the global population—he merely moves from one spot on the planet to another.

But will the current crop of immigrants acculturate? Immigrants to America always have. Some critics, like Mr. Buchanan, claim that this time, it's different. Mexicans seem to draw his particular ire, probably because they are currently our largest single source of immigration.

Yet only about a fifth (22 percent) of legal immigrants to

America currently come from Mexico. Adding illegal immigrants might boost the figure to 30 percent, but the proportion of Mexican immigrants will almost surely shrink over time. Mexican fertility has diminished from 6.5 children per woman 30 years ago to 2.5 children now, and continues to fall. If high immigration continues under such circumstances, Mexico will run out of Mexicans.

California hosts a wide variety of immigrant groups in addition to Mexicans. And the children and grandchildren of Koreans, Chinese, Khmer, Russian Jews, Iranians, and Thai (to name a few) will speak English, not Spanish. Even among Mexican-Americans, many second- and third-generation offspring speak no Spanish at all, often to the dismay of their elders (a familiar American story).

Michael Barone's book *The New Americans* theorizes that Mexican immigrants are following roughly the same course of earlier Italian and Irish immigrants. Noel Ignatiev's book *How the Irish Became White* notes that it took a hundred years until Irish-Americans (who were routinely characterized as drunken "gorillas") reached full income parity with the rest of America.

California has repealed its bilingual education programs. Nearly half of Latino voters supported the proposition, even though it was demonized by opponents as being anti-Hispanic. Latina mothers reportedly tell their children, with no intent to disparage the Spanish language, that "Spanish is the language of busboys"—stressing that in America you have to speak English to get ahead.

Immigrants Are Eventually Accepted

The huge immigration wave at the dawn of the twentieth century undeniably brought tumult to America. Many early social scientists promoted theories of what is now called "scientific racism," which "proved" that persons from Northwest Europe were biologically superior. The new immigrants—Jews, Poles, and Italians—were considered racially apart and far down the totem pole of human character and intelligence. Blacks and Asians were hardly worth measuring. The immigration wave sparked a resurgence of the Ku Klux Klan (KKK), peaking in the early 1920s. At that time, the biggest KKK state was not in the South; it was Indiana, where Catholics, Jews, and immigrants, as well as blacks, were targets.

Francis Walker, superintendent of the U.S. Bureau of the

Census in the late 1890s, and later president of Massachusetts Institute of Technology (MIT), wrote in 1896 that "The entrance of such vast masses of peasantry degraded below our utmost conceptions is a matter which no intelligent patriot can look upon without the gravest apprehension and alarm. They are beaten men from beaten races. They have none of the ideas and aptitudes such as belong to those who were descended from the tribes that met under the oak trees of old Germany to make laws and choose chiefs." (Sorry, Francis, but Germany did not have a good twentieth century.)

> **❝** *Our immigrants, who come to our land by choice, are our best salesmen.* **❞**

Fast-forward to the present. By high margins, Americans now tell pollsters it was a very good thing that Poles, Italians, and Jews emigrated to America. Once again, it's the newcomers who are viewed with suspicion. This time, it's the Mexicans, Filipinos, and people from the Caribbean who make Americans nervous. But such views change over time. The newer immigrant groups are typically more popular now than they were even a decade ago.

Look at the high rates of intermarriage. Most Americans have long since lost their qualms about marriage between people of different European ethnicities. That is spreading across new boundaries. In 1990, 64 percent of Asian Americans married outside their heritage, as did 37 percent of Hispanics. Black-white intermarriage is much lower, but it climbed from 3 percent in 1980 to 9 percent in 1998. (One reason to do away with the race question on the census is that within a few decades we won't be able to know who's what.)

Can the West, led by America, prevail in a world full of sometimes unfriendly neighbors? Substantial numbers of people are necessary (though not sufficient) for a country, or a civilization, to be globally influential. Will America and its Western allies have enough people to keep their ideas and principles alive?

On the surface, it doesn't look good. In 1986, I wrote a book called *The Birth Dearth*. My thesis was that birth rates in developed parts of the world—Europe, North America, Australia, and Japan, nations where liberal Western values are rooted—had sunk so low that there was danger ahead. At that time, women in those modern countries were bearing a lifetime average of 1.83 children, the lowest rate ever absent war, famine, economic depression, or epidemic illness. It was, in fact, 15 percent below the longterm population replacement level.

Those trendlines have now plummeted even further. Today [2002], the fertility rate in the modern countries averages 1.5 children per woman, 28 percent below the replacement level. The European rate, astonishingly, is 1.34 children per woman—radically below replacement level. The Japanese rate is similar. The United States is the exceptional country in the current demographic scene.

As a whole, the nations of the Western world will soon be less populous, and a substantially smaller fraction of the world population. Demographer Samuel Preston estimates that even if European fertility rates jump back to replacement level immediately (which won't happen) the continent would still lose 100 million people by 2060. Should the rate not level off fairly soon, the ramifications are incalculable, or, as the Italian demographer Antonio Golini likes to mutter at demographic meetings, "unsustainable . . . unsustainable." (Shockingly, the current Italian fertility rate is 1.2 children per woman, and it has been at or below 1.5 for 20 years—a full generation.)

> *[Immigration] can keep us strong enough to defend and perhaps extend our views and values.*

The modern countries of the world, the bearers of Western civilization, made up one third of the global population in 1950, and one fifth in 2000, and are projected to represent one eighth by 2050. If we end up in a world with nine competing civilizations, as [political scientist] Samuel Huntington maintains, this will make it that much harder for Western values to prevail in the cultural and political arenas.

The good news is that fertility rates have also plunged in the less developed countries—from 6 children in 1970 to 2.9 today. By the middle to end of [the twenty-first] century, there should be a rough global convergence of fertility rates and population growth.

America Should Encourage Immigration

Since [the September 11, 2001, terrorist attacks on America] immigration has gotten bad press in America. The terrorist villains, indeed, were foreigners. Not only in the U.S. but in many other nations as well, governments are suddenly cracking down on illegal entry. This is understandable for the moment. But an enduring turn away from legal immigration would be foolhardy for America and its allies.

If America doesn't continue to take in immigrants, it won't continue to grow in the long run. If the Europeans and Japanese don't start to accept more immigrants they will evaporate. Who will empty the bedpans in Italy's retirement homes? The only major pool of immigrants available to Western countries hails from the less developed world, i.e. non-white, and non-Western countries.

The West as a whole is in a deep demographic ditch. Accordingly, Western countries should try to make it easier for couples who want to have children. In America, the advent of tax credits for children (which went from zero to $1,000 per child per year over the last decade) is a small step in the direction of fertility reflation. Some European nations are enacting similar pro-natal policies. But their fertility rates are so low, and their economies so constrained, that any such actions can only be of limited help.

That leaves immigration. I suggest America should make immigration safer (by more carefully investigating new entrants), but not cut it back. It may even be wise to make a small increase in our current immigration rate. America needs to keep growing, and we can fruitfully use both high- and low-skill immigrants. Pluralism works here, as it does in Canada and Australia.

Can pluralism work in Europe? I don't know, and neither do the Europeans. They hate the idea, but they will depopulate if they don't embrace pluralism, via immigration. Perhaps our example can help Europeans see that pluralism might work in the admittedly more complex European context. Japan is probably a hopeless case; perhaps the Japanese should just change the name of their country to Dwindle.

Our non-pluralist Western allies will likely diminish in population, relative power, and influence during [the twenty-first] century. They will become much grayer. Nevertheless, by 2050 there will still be 750 million of them left, so the U.S. needs to keep the Western alliance strong. For all our bickering, let us not forget that the European story in the second half of the twentieth century was a wonderful one: Western Europeans stopped killing each other. Now they are joining hands politically. The next big prize may be Russia. If the Russians choose our path, we will see what [nineteenth-century French political theorist Alexis de] Tocqueville saw: that America and Russia are natural allies.

We must enlist other allies as well. America and India, for instance, are logical partners—pluralist, large, English-speaking, and democratic. We must tell our story. And our immigrants, who come to our land by choice, are our best salesmen. We should extend our radio services to the Islamic world, as we have to the unliberated nations of Asia through Radio Free Asia. The people at the microphones will be U.S. immigrants.

Public Diplomacy

We can lose the contest of civilizations if the developing countries don't evolve toward Western values. One of the best forms of "public diplomacy" is immigration. New immigrants send money home, bypassing corrupt governments—the best kind of foreign aid there is. They go back home to visit and tell their families and friends in the motherland that American modernism, while not perfect, ain't half-bad. Some return home permanently, but they bring with them Western expectations of open government, economic efficiency, and personal liberty. They know that Westernism need not be restricted to the West, and they often have an influence on local politics when they return to their home countries.

Still, because of Europe and Japan, the demographic slide of Western civilization will continue. And so, America must be prepared to go it alone. If we keep admitting immigrants at our current levels there will be almost 400 million Americans by 2050. That can keep us strong enough to defend and perhaps extend our views and values. And the civilization we will be advancing may not just be Western, but even more universal: American.

9

Immigration Contributes to America's Decline

Patrick J. Buchanan

Patrick J. Buchanan, an adviser to three American presidents, ran for the Republican nomination for president in 1992 and 1996. He was also the Reform Party's presidential candidate in 2000. The author of five books including the best sellers Right from the Beginning *and* A Republic, Not an Empire, *he is a syndicated columnist and a founding member of three of America's foremost public affairs shows:* The McLaughlin Group, The Capital Gang, *and* Crossfire.

White Americans may soon become a minority as the number of foreign-born inhabitants grows larger every year. America faces a growing number of uneducated, poverty-stricken immigrants from third world countries, many of whom enter the country illegally and end up in prison, eating up tax dollars. America also faces the larger cultural problem of how to define itself as a nation. Traditionally, nations have been defined as a group of people who share a common language, ancestry, traditions, and religion. As more people of various nationalities, beliefs, and mores enter America, Americans have less and less in common with one another. Some people argue that a shared belief in a country's founding principles defines a nation. However, poor turnouts at elections reveal how little Americans revere their country's tenets. Millions of immigrants with disparate beliefs and values are unlikely to repair America's disunion.

Patrick J. Buchanan, *The Death of the West: How Dying Populations and Immigrant Invasions Imperil Our Country and Civilization.* New York: Thomas Dunne Books, an imprint of St. Martin's Press, 2002. Copyright © 2002 by Patrick J. Buchanan. All rights reserved. Reproduced by permission of St. Martin's Press, LLC.

America is no longer the biracial society of 1960 that struggled to erase divisions and close gaps in a nation 90 percent white. Today we juggle the rancorous and rival claims of a multiracial, multiethnic, and multicultural country. [Former] Vice President Gore captured the new America in his famous howler, when he translated our national slogan, "E Pluribus Unum," backward, as "Out of one, many."

Today there are 28.4 million foreign-born in the United States. Half are from Latin America and the Caribbean, a fourth from Asia. The rest are from Africa, the Middle East, and Europe. One in every five New Yorkers and Floridians is foreign-born, as is one of every four Californians. With 8.4 million foreign-born, and not one new power plant built in a decade, small wonder California faces power shortages and power outages. With endless immigration, America is going to need an endless expansion of its power sources—hydroelectric power, fossil fuels (oil, coal, gas), and nuclear power. The only alternative is blackouts, brownouts, and endless lines at the pump.

> **❝** *Today there are 28.4 million foreign-born in the United States.* **❞**

In the 1990s, immigrants and their children were responsible for 100 percent of the population growth of California, New York, New Jersey, Illinois, and Massachusetts, and over half the population growth of Florida, Texas, Michigan, and Maryland. As the United States allots most of its immigrant visas to relatives of new arrivals, it is difficult for Europeans to come, while entire villages from El Salvador are now here.

The results of the Third World bias in immigration can be seen in our social statistics. The median age of Euro-Americans is 36; for Hispanics, it is 26. The median age of all foreign-born, 33, is far below that of the older American ethnic groups, such as English, 40, and Scots-Irish, 43. These social statistics raise a question: Is the U.S. government, by deporting scarcely 1 percent of an estimated eleven million illegal aliens each year, failing in its constitutional duty to protect the rights of American citizens? Consider:

- A third of the legal immigrants who come to the United States have not finished high school. Some 22 percent do not even have a ninth-grade education, compared to less than 5 percent of our native born.

- Over 36 percent of all immigrants, and 57 percent of those from Central America, do not earn twenty thousand dollars a year. Of the immigrants who have come since 1980, 60 percent still do not earn twenty thousand dollars a year.
- Of immigrant households in the United States, 29 percent are below the poverty line, twice the 14 percent of native born.
- Immigrant use of food stamps, Supplemental Social Security, and school lunch programs runs from 50 percent to 100 percent higher than use by native born.
- Mr. Clinton's Department of Labor estimated that 50 percent of the real-wage losses sustained by low-income Americans is due to immigration.
- By 1991, foreign nationals accounted for 24 percent of all arrests in Los Angeles and 36 percent of all arrests in Miami.
- In 1980, federal and state prisons housed nine thousand criminal aliens. By 1995, this had soared to fifty-nine thousand criminal aliens, a figure that does not include aliens who became citizens or the criminals sent over by Castro in the Mariel boat lift.
- Between 1988 and 1994, the number of illegal aliens in California's prisons more than tripled from fifty-five hundred to eighteen thousand.

None of the above statistics, however, holds for emigrants from Europe. And some of the statistics, on low education, for example, do not apply to emigrants from Asia.

> *Common principles of government are not enough to hold us together.*

Nevertheless, mass emigration from poor Third World countries is "good for business," especially businesses that employ large numbers at low wages. In the spring of 2001, the Business Industry Political Action Committee, BIPAC, issued "marching orders for grass-roots mobilization." The *Wall Street Journal* said that the 400 blue-chip companies and 150 trade associations "will call for continued normalization of trade with China . . . and easing immigration restrictions to meet labor needs. . . ." But what is good for corporate America is not necessarily good for Middle America. When it comes to open borders, the corporate interest and the national interest do not coincide, they collide. Should America suffer a sustained recession, we will find out if the melting pot is still working.

But mass immigration raises more critical issues than jobs or wages, for immigration is ultimately about America herself.

What Is a Nation?

Most of the people who leave their homelands to come to America, whether from Mexico or Mauritania, are good people, decent people. They seek the same better life our ancestors sought when they came. They come to work; they obey our laws; they cherish our freedoms; they relish the opportunities the greatest nation on earth has to offer; most love America; many wish to become part of the American family. One may encounter these newcomers everywhere. But the record number of foreign-born coming from cultures with little in common with Americans raises a different question: What is a nation?

Some define a nation as one people of common ancestry, language, literature, history, heritage, heroes, traditions, customs, mores, and faith who have lived together over time on the same land under the same rulers. This is the blood-and-soil idea of a nation. Among those who pressed this definition were Secretary of State John Quincy Adams, who laid down these conditions on immigrants: "They must cast off the European skin, never to resume it. They must look forward to their posterity rather than backward to their ancestors." Theodore Roosevelt, who thundered against "hyphenated-Americanism," seemed to share Adams's view. Woodrow Wilson, speaking to newly naturalized Americans in 1915 in Philadelphia, echoed T.R.: "A man who thinks of himself as belonging to a particular national group in America has yet to become an American." This idea, of Americans as a separate and unique people, was first given expression by John Jay in *Federalist 2:*

> Providence has been pleased to give this one connected country to one united people—a people descended from the same ancestors, speaking the same language, professing the same religion, at-

tached to the same principles of government, very
similar in their manners and customs, and who,
by their joint counsels, arms, and efforts, fighting
side by side throughout a long and bloody war,
have nobly established their general liberty and
independence.

But can anyone say today that we Americans are "one united
people"?

We are not descended from the same ancestors. We no
longer speak the same language. We do not profess the same religion. We are no longer simply Protestant, Catholic, and Jewish, as sociologist Will Herberg described us in his *Essay in American Religious Sociology* in 1955. We are now Protestant, Catholic,
Jewish, Mormon, Muslim, Hindu, Buddhist, Taoist, Shintoist,
Santeria, New Age, voodoo, agnostic, atheist, humanist, Rasta-
farian, and Wiccan. Even the mention of Jesus' name at the In-
auguration by the preachers Mr. Bush selected to give the invo-
cations evoked fury and cries of "insensitive," "divisive," and
"exclusionary." A *New Republic* editorial lashed out at these
"crushing Christological thuds" from the Inaugural stand. We
no longer agree on whether God exists, when life begins, and
what is moral and immoral. We are not "similar in our manners
and customs." We never fought "side by side throughout a long
and bloody war." The Greatest Generation did, but it is passing
away. If the rest of us recall a "long and bloody war," it was Vietnam, and, no, we were not side by side.

We remain "attached to the same principles of government."
But common principles of government are not enough to hold
us together. The South was "attached to the same principles of
government" as the North. But that did not stop Southerners
from fighting four years of bloody war to be free of their North-
ern brethren.

The American Creed

In his Inaugural, President Bush rejected Jay's vision: "America
has never been united by blood or birth or soil. We are bound
by ideals that move us beyond our background, lift us above
our interests, and teach us what it means to be a citizen." In his
The Disuniting of America, Arthur Schlesinger subscribes to the
Bush idea of a nation, united by shared belief in an American
Creed to be found in our history and greatest documents: the

Declaration of Independence, the Constitution, and the Get-tysburg Address. Writes Schlesinger:

> The American Creed envisages a nation composed of individuals making their own choices and accountable to themselves, not a nation based on inviolable ethnic communities. For our values are not matters or whim and happenstance. History has given them to us. They are anchored in our national experience, in our great national documents, in our national heroes, in our folkways, our traditions, and standards. [Our values] work for us; and, for that reason, we live and die by them.

But Americans no longer agree on values, history, or heroes. What one-half of America sees as a glorious past the other views as shameful and wicked. Columbus, Washington, Jefferson, Jackson, Lincoln, and Lee—all of them heroes of the old America—are all under attack. Those most American of words, equality and freedom, today hold different meanings for different Americans. As for our "great national documents," the Supreme Court decisions that interpret our Constitution have not united us; for forty years they have divided us, bitterly, over prayer in school, integration, busing, flag burning, abortion, pornography, and the Ten Commandments.

Nor is a belief in democracy sufficient to hold us together. Half of the nation did not even bother to vote in the presidential election of 2000; three out of five do not vote in off-year elections. Millions cannot name their congressman, senators, or the Supreme Court justices. They do not care.

Whether one holds to the blood-and-soil idea of a nation, or to the creedal idea, or both, neither nation is what it was in the 1940s, 1950s, or 1960s. We live in the same country, we are governed by the same leaders, but can we truly say we are still one nation and one people?

It is hard to say yes, harder to believe that over a million immigrants every year, from every country on earth, a third of them breaking in, will reforge the bonds of our disuniting nation. John Stuart Mill warned that "free institutions are next to impossible in a country made up of different nationalities. Among a people without fellow-feeling, especially if they read and speak different languages, the united public opinion necessary to the working of representative government cannot exist."

We are about to find out if Mill was right.

10

American Culture Has Become More Angry and Dangerous

Timothy W. Maier

Timothy W. Maier is an investigative reporter for Insight on the News, *a member of the congressional press galleries and Investigative Reporters and Editors, an organization that provides educational services to parties interested in investigative journalism; and a frequent guest on national television and radio shows.*

From violent post office workers to enraged soccer moms, more Americans are losing control of their anger than ever before. The recent growth in nationwide anger-management workshops, violence institutes, and self-help guides to controlling rage reveal that the number of people throwing temper tantrums is on the upswing. Some theorists argue that a desire to win at all costs is behind the increase in anger while others contend that low self-esteem fuels out-of-control rage. Still others maintain that anger problems are biochemical in origin. Regardless of the cause, researchers agree that anger can be controlled through anger-management workshops, relaxation, meditation, or massage therapy. Accepting that life may not always go as planned, however, is the best way to reduce the possibility of losing control.

It began on a rural road in Wisconsin when my rusty 1982 Datsun nearly was broadsided by a truck. Fortunately I quickly hit my horn and the driver slammed on his brakes.

Checking the rearview mirror while continuing down the road I could see the truck was accelerating rapidly until it was tailgating dangerously at a 50 mph clip.

A stoplight was ahead, maybe 50 yards. Should I run it and risk a ticket, or should I stop? I stopped—and as I did I saw the U.S. government emblem on the truck that screeched to a halt behind me. A uniformed 30-something man stepped out and approached as I rolled down the window.

"Oh, my God! He's a postal worker and you can bet he's not trying to deliver my mail," I thought. The man's face was beet red and his shoulders were trembling with fury as he screamed, "I put up with you people all day long! I don't need you to honk at me!" In another second he had run back to his truck and sped off to deliver the mail.

That was more than a decade ago. Not long afterward, postal employees started getting a bad rap for flipping out and "going postal." Today, it's not just disgruntled mail carriers who are giving way to unbridled furies but next-door neighbors, baby-sitters, PTA mothers and even kids. At the World Trade Organization, or WTO, conference in Seattle, angry protesters outraged at the Clinton international agenda were silenced by police in body armor deploying tear gas and firing rubber bullets to disperse the crowds.

A Mad World

One man's stress is another man's living. It has become a mad world with nationwide anger-management workshops, angry people checking into places such as the Violence Institute of Chicago and bookstores stacked with self-help guides like Mary LoVerde's *Stop Screaming at the Microwave* and Richard Carlson's best-selling *Don't Sweat the Small Stuff.* Amusing reads, but not many seem to be incorporating that "Don't worry, be happy" philosophy into their daily lives. The WTO demonstrators certainly weren't.

"Those people in Seattle, they're just saying, 'I don't want to be a little cog in the machine, I don't want all these world leaders controlling my economic fate,'" says "Stress Doc" Mark Gorkin, a psychotherapist and motivational humorist on America Online, formerly a stress and violence-prevention consultant to the U.S. Postal Service.

It's no longer just outrage in America, Gorkin says, it's rage of all kinds. Who but horror writer Stephen King could have imagined a suburban Alabama mother fatally shooting another mom in a road-rage incident or presidential contenders facing questions about airline rage? Even the office isn't a safe haven. In a span of four months, July to November [1999], shooting sprees broke out at Seattle's Northlake Shipyard (two dead); Xerox Corp. in Honolulu (seven dead); an Atlanta office complex (nine dead); and in Pelham, Ala. (three dead).

"Civility is on the decline," euphemizes James V. O'Conner, founder of the Cuss Control Academy in Northbrook, Ill., which works to teach people—from children to senior citizens—not to use the seven dirty words. "What we have become," he says "is a nation of whiners and complainers. We have to accept facts: Accidents happen and things go wrong," and none of it is improved one bit by repeating the swearing cliches.

> *It's no longer just outrage in America . . . it's rage of all kinds.*

Trouble is that this lack of civility, supported by vulgarity, has spilled from the streets and offices to the rest of our culture. In September [1999], hip-hop artist and producer Puffy Combs was ordered to participate in an anger-management class after he beat a fellow record producer. Anger even received a major pop-culture nod in February [1999] when an episode of Fox's *The Simpsons* focused on Marge Simpson's experiences with road rage and its aftermath.

Marge, the matriarch of the dysfunctional cartoon clan, found herself stuck behind a funeral procession while driving the family's new sport-utility vehicle. Though usually level-headed, she cut around the procession, screaming, "Get that corpse off the road! The streets are for the living!" She was apprehended and sent to traffic school to learn to deal with her road rage. "So when you go out for a drive," Sgt. Crew, the course instructor, told students, "remember to leave your murderous anger where it belongs—at home."

And anger even has reached U.S. sporting events, as fans have sunk almost to the level of Europe's soccer fanatics. In Milwaukee a disgruntled Brewers fan jumped from the stands to take a swing at the Philadelphia Phillies' right fielder. In Philadelphia, fans showed their contempt by tossing radio batteries at players, prompting authorities to install a municipal judge at Veteran's Stadium to provide timely justice. In Washington, a soccer fan stabbed another during a close D.C. United match. In Denver, fans rocked Oakland Raiders football players with snowballs and a player charged the stands to confront the attackers during a Monday Night Football game. Even golf's Ryder Cup has seen its share of rowdy fans, and at the Preakness in Baltimore a disturbed man ran onto the track to attack a jockey.

> ❝*Anger even has reached U.S. sporting events.*❞

The *Washington Post* recently editorialized that it is the desire to win at all costs that leads to this fan pandemonium. Perhaps the same can he said of the sport of politics. GOP presidential hopeful John McCain's anger has been the subject of repeated attacks, although presidents Lyndon Johnson, Dwight Eisenhower, Richard Nixon and even Harry Truman also were known to throw tantrums. And don't forget Bill Clinton. As McCain explained to CNBC's *Hardball* in September [1999], "I used to lose [my temper] . . . all the time. Every time I lost it, either in captivity or out, I said something I regretted, usually harming someone." Now, he added, "I not only count to 10, every day I get up and pray, 'I don't want to lose my temper today.'". . .

Looking for Answers

While McCain plays down his anger, America itself seems to be getting more cranky by the hour. And this despite low unemployment, increasing longevity, unprecedented affluence and technology that increasingly seems capable of almost anything. Why?

People are out of control because they have low self-esteem, suggests Marilyn J. Sorensen, a psychologist in Portland, Ore., who wrote *Breaking the Chain of Low Self-Esteem*. High taxes, lying politicians, traffic jams and exhausting schedules all are culprits, she says. "The demands are endless and people have no time to themselves or quality time with their families." Some people feel powerless, she continues. "Many work all their lives and have little to show for it." Those with no money to invest don't benefit from the booming stock market; indeed, they "feel even more like they have missed out; they feel further behind and know they can never catch up."

Prosperity also has its disadvantages, says the Stress Doc. "People wind up staying in positions longer than they should and they become burnt up or burnt out," he says. "They put in a lot of overtime and we live in this new 24/7, 365-day global and computer economy where people have lost how to communicate with each other."

Gorkin has quite a list of culprits. "E-mail has stopped people from talking to each other," he adds. "E-mail is really Escape-mail. People can avoid each other by sending out a blistering note that they wouldn't dare say face to face. We have created a division of the Roman Empire—the world of haves and have-nots—of those who are computer-savvy and those intimidated by the new revolution. Salesmen resent the e-commerce. It is bringing a new death of the salesman."

When the computer crashes, all hell breaks loose because then people have to confront each other, says Gorkin. But the serious study of growing popular anger predates the computer revolution. Charles Speilberger of the University of South Florida tells *Insight* that modern research of the problem began 20 years ago when cardiologists developed the concept of "type A" personalities. "It turns out type A behavior was linked to heart disease, but the lethal component of type A personality was anger," says Speilberger.

> *We are a nation living on the edge.*

The Florida academic distinguishes between feeling anger and expressing anger. As bad as expressing anger is proving to be for the society at large, Speilberger's studies show anger turned inward, which leads to depression, has deeply destructive physical consequences leading to elevated blood pressure and hypertension, heart attack and stroke.

If keeping your cool is so good for you, why do people lose it? Because, for one thing, "the promise of service never equals reality," notes C. Leslie Charles, who recently wrote *Why Is Everyone so Cranky?* and has made it a mission to stamp out anger with her "cranky buster" buttons and T-shirts. "We are overwhelmed, overworked, overscheduled and overspent," she declares. "We are a nation living on the edge."

Or, as she puts it in her book, "giving has become secondary to getting." The got-to-have-it mentality, she says, has soured the nation's collective mood. "On our streets and highways, in our workplaces and even in our homes, we've abandoned common courtesy," she writes. People are "impatient, rude and demanding." And it's not one thing that got us there, either, she insists. "It isn't the big things that push us over the edge. It's the succession of little things that keep building."

Sound familiar? In the 1980s the late actor Peter Finch made famous the line, "I'm as mad as hell and I'm not going to take it anymore," in his Oscar-winning movie *Network*. The Finch character had the entire city of New York screaming the same line.

Recognize Yourself?

Do you want to know if you are on the road to that kind of madness? Charles says you might be if you tend to insist that you are entitled to what you want when you want it, are determined to be impatient or rude when other people are behaving stupidly or tend to insist furiously that since your time is important you should not have to be inconvenienced by others. If you recognize yourself, she says, it might be a good time to seek professional help or read her book.

"It's what we do with our anger or how we express it that matters," Charles says. "There is a healthy way to express anger, such as Candy Lightner did when her daughter was killed by a drunk driver. She started Mothers Against Drunk Driving. We should have a road-rage advocate group." Instead, people dwell on what they don't have, Charles says. Our "expectation machine" with its impossible-to-deliver promises insists that life is like sports: "There are winners and losers, and if you are not a winner guess what you are?"

Our crankiness, she writes, is the "natural by-product of our social compulsion to drive the right car, live in the right home in the right area with all the right furnishings, have the right job, send our kids to the right day care or school, wear the right clothes and accessories, belong to the right clubs and go to the right vacation spots." Believing that having the best means we are the best leads to the anxiety that results from financial instability. "Many of us are so busy trying to create the right life that we've turned our existence into a nightmare of debt."

While Charles blames our culture of greed, pop psychologist David Weiner says the culprit is biochemical. In other words, our brains are out of whack, he tells *Insight*. It's all about battling our "inner dummy" he says. Of course, he would say that. He wrote a book called *Battling the Inner Dummy*, referring to what he claims is a malfunctioning component in the modern brain. According to Weiner, the physical brain hasn't changed in 300,000 years, but our demands on it have. "If we could get in there with a screwdriver like we do with defective software, we would be ahead of the game."

> *Employees who are angry create a hostile work environment and tend to do only just enough work to get by.*

If you want to see if you are winning the battle against anger, take Weiner's power-drive test. "Very few people have an organ in their brains that may be out of balance, and most people are in the middle on the test. The problem is not in the middle, but if you have a kid with a genetic predisposition and with a nine power-program score and a kid who shows little guilt and fear, and even though his parents may be Quakers, you got a kid who might go to the school and shoot someone."

Simmer Down

Others say that while an angry disposition tends to be inherited, it can be overcome. "Our experience is that when people can identify their anger from the past as causing problems in the present, and we get rid of it in the right way, other problems of everyday life then can be solved," says Mitchell Messer of the Violence Institute of Chicago. "And they can even be solved if our brains are on fire."

The Violence Institute uses Adlerian psychology, which presumes that people "overcompensate" for feelings of inferiority and inadequacy in childhood. "Not only do we feel inferior and inadequate to cope in childhood, but it turns out we blame ourselves. That will tie you up in knots," says Messer, "and it will give us preexisting anger in our bloodstream so that all it will take is 2 ounces to spill us over." The only people to escape this, he notes, "are American citizens with perfect parents."

The young shooters, like everyone else, have been suppressing anger for years, says Messer. "When they cannot take the pressure any more, all of a sudden, 19 and behold, they turn it outward. What did you think they would do?"

Recent studies show it may not only be the angry child we need to be concerned about, but also coworkers. Take a look at the people in nearby cubicles and remember that while homicides committed during robberies declined during the nineties, killings by coworkers rose dramatically.

Donald Gibson, a professor at the Yale University School of Management, says the recent spate of workplace violence is not surprising. Coauthor of *The Experience of Anger at Work: Lessons From the Chronically Angry*, Gibson notes that nearly 25 percent of respondents to a 1996 Gallup telephone survey of 1,000 adults indicated that they were "generally at least somewhat angry at work." Much of that discontent is coming from the East Coast, where 12 percent of the respondents called themselves quite angry, compared with 6 percent in the Midwest, 4 percent in the South and 3 percent in the West.

As for what makes them mad, 11 percent of those questioned claimed the actions of supervisors or managers as the No. 1 reason they get upset. Nine percent of respondents cited others not being productive and tight deadlines or a heavy workload, while still others pointed to a public that treats them badly as the root of their stress.

"Supervisors need to think about how they are communicating with employees," Gibson says, because the effect of workplace anger can be quite costly for corporations. Employees who are angry create a hostile work environment and tend to do only just enough work to get by, he says.

New Jersey psychologists Steven Dranoff and Wanda Dobrich blame the rise of anger in America on "displacement" aggression: A father comes home from work and yells at his wife, who snaps at her son, who then kicks the dog. And there are other causes. The popular wisdom appears to be that 1970s deinstitutionalization of mental patients, combined with a managed-care health system in crisis, has produced too little help for those who need it the most. Talk about mad as hell— *Newsweek* magazine described the health-care system as HMO Hell. A *Newsweek/Discovery* survey revealed that 61 percent of Americans polled were frustrated and angry—about their health insurance. "Managed care is eroding care and . . . you are left with how to deal with the situation with no counselors or shrinks," Dranoff says. On top of that, Dobrich adds, more women are entering the workforce and men and women are having to learn how to relate to each other in a new workforce culture. It's not going too well, according to the U.S. Equal Employment Opportunity Commission, which reported a 300 percent rise in coworker sexual-harassment complaints this year.

Interestingly, there is not much difference between the sexes in feelings of anger, says Speilberger, but major differences in the way anger is expressed. "Most women rarely feel like expressing anger physically . . . they express it verbally," he says. "Men don't discriminate so much between screaming at someone and hitting them. For women, there's a big difference."

While Dranoff and Dobrich see a solution in anger workshops, others have sought alternative sublimation. For example, Candace Talmadge, a Texas woman who says she used to suffer from an anger problem, turned to "Sunan Therapy," which emphasizes using meditation to find a "happy place." Perhaps reflecting a self-esteem issue, a relieved Talmadge says, "I always thought people were saying I was the worst slime that ever existed, but not anymore." Therapist Jana Simons sees this new-age fix between therapist and client as "two explorers using love energy" to get in touch with the "mental, physical, emotional and spiritual belief systems." And all on a massage table at $100 a session.

If you're not quite ready for the massage table, counseling or brain surgery, *Cranky* author Charles offers advice: "Take a bite of reality. Flights will be delayed, even canceled—endure it. You will be inconvenienced—count on it. People are going to do things that irritate you—expect it. Uncontrollables are part of life—accept it. These hassles won't change, but you can."

11

America Has Become a Culture of Cheaters

David Callahan

David Callahan is cofounder of the public policy center Demos, where he is director of research. He is the author of many books and is a frequent commentator on television and radio. His articles have appeared in many publications, including the New York Times, *the* Washington Post, *and* USA Today.

Record numbers of Americans are cheating to get ahead academically, financially, and professionally. Students cheat to be accepted to good colleges, people steal music via file-sharing software, people cheat on their taxes, and athletes take steroids to outperform their competitors. In the past quarter century, people have become even more focused on making money. In addition, income gaps among Americans have skyrocketed and fewer people control more of the nation's wealth. These cultural changes have led to more cheating because, as income gaps increase, Americans face new pressures, such as heightened competition at work and school, to succeed. In fact, there are now bigger rewards for cheating and the temptation is everywhere. Moreover, lower-income citizens are more inclined to cheat when they see corporate leaders are rarely punished for cheating. America needs to have a serious conversation about cheating, but finding solutions to America's cheating culture will not be easy.

[There is] a pattern of widespread cheating throughout U.S. society. By its nature cheating is intended to go undetected, and trends in unethical behavior are hard to document. Still, available evidence strongly suggests that Americans are not only cheating more in many areas but are also feeling less guilty about it. When "everybody does it," or imagines that everybody does it, a cheating culture has emerged.

Yet why all the cheating, and why now?

Watchdogs of Virtue

One might think that there'd be no shortage of possible explanations floating around for this crisis. America has been a nation of moralizers since the days of Benjamin Franklin, who advised in his 13 Virtues to "Imitate Jesus and Socrates"—a pretty high bar. But rarely has that cultural leaning been more pronounced than in recent decades. We have been living in the age of the Moral Majority and the Christian Coalition, the age of family values and zero tolerance. Religious figures and intellectuals and newspaper columnists have talked endlessly in recent years about moral issues large and small: teen pregnancy, school uniforms, violent video games, graffiti, pedophilia, welfare dependency, crime, drug use, and so forth. God, who previously didn't play much of a role in American politics, has come to be as omnipresent in election campaigns as corporate donors seeking favors.

Yet America's watchdogs of virtue have been largely silent about the new epidemic of cheating. To be sure, rampant cheating by students has begun to receive attention in the past several years. And the recent corporate scandals induced a media feeding frenzy. There have also been big stories about cheating by athletes, or tax evasion, or plagiarism by journalists. Still, there's been very little effort to connect all these dots and see them for what they represent: a profound moral crisis that reflects deep economic and social problems in American society.

Concerns about cheating do not jibe easily with the way that Americans have talked about values and personal responsibility since the early 1980s. That conversation has been orchestrated by conservatives and the religious right, while liberals—often uncomfortable talking about values—have largely kept their mouths shut. America's moral ills were defined in the '80s and '90s in terms that reflected traditional conservative worries, with a focus on things like crime, drugs, premarital sex, and divorce. Other concerns—little problems like greed, envy, materialism, and inequality—have been excluded from the values debate.

But lately conservatives haven't had much to complain about. Many aspects of Americans' personal behavior have changed in recent years. Crime is down. Teenage pregnancy is down. Drunk driving is down. Abortion is down. The use of tobacco and illicit drugs is down. Opinion surveys suggest that Americans are growing more concerned about personal responsibility, as conservatives have narrowly defined that term.

Nevertheless, cheating is up. Cheating is everywhere. By cheating I mean breaking the rules to get ahead academically, professionally, or financially. Some of this cheating involves violating the law; some does not. Either way, most of it is by people who, on the whole, view themselves as upstanding members of society. Again and again, Americans who wouldn't so much as shoplift a pack of chewing gum are committing felonies at tax time, betraying the trust of their patients, misleading investors, ripping off their insurance company, or lying to their clients.

> *// Americans are not only cheating more in many areas but are also feeling less guilty about it. //*

Something strange is going on here. Americans seem to be using two moral compasses. One directs our behavior when it comes to things like sex, family, drugs, and traditional forms of crime. A second provides us ethical guidance in the realm of career, money, and success.

The obvious question is: Where did we pick up that second compass? . . .

Someone Can Always Get Rich

In 1981, after he was sworn in as President, Ronald Reagan pronounced: "Government is not the solution, government is the problem." Elsewhere, Reagan articulated another adage that summed up both his philosophy and the dawning ethos of the time: "What I want to see above all is that this remains a country where someone can always get rich."

Ronald Reagan's election stands as a historic turning point that helped crystallize and accelerate emerging trends in American society. Government activism was out. Making money was in. And over the next twenty years, the ideas and values associated with the free market would reign in U.S. society with more influence than at any time since the Gilded Age. "By the end of 2000," wrote one observer, "the market as the dominant cultural force had so infiltrated society that it is increasingly difficult to remember any other reality."

> *Americans who wouldn't so much as shoplift a pack of chewing gum are committing felonies at tax time.*

This seismic change has altered the terms of American life. First, thanks to America's laissez-faire revolution, a focus on money and the bottom line has swept into areas that previously were insulated from market pressures. Partly this has been a good thing. Consumers have more choices and get better service these days, and we have an economy that nurtures innovation and entrepreneurialism. Yet there's been a cost. More people in more occupations are chasing money—or being chased by bean counters.

Second, income gaps among Americans have soared over the past quarter century. When profits and performance are the only measure of success, old-fashioned ideas about fairness go out the window. Lean-and-mean business strategies have conspired with trends like globalization and technological change to ensure huge income gains by well-educated professionals— while many less-skilled workers have been running in place or losing ground. Fewer people also control more of the nation's wealth. In fact, the top 1 percent of households have more wealth than the entire bottom 90 percent combined. Economic inequality has led to striking changes in our society.

• In America's new winner-take-all society there is infinitely more to gain, and to lose, when it comes to getting into the right college, getting the right job, becoming a "hot" reporter, showing good earnings on Wall Street, having a high batting average, or otherwise becoming a star achiever.

• Higher inequality has led to more divisions between Americans and weakened the social fabric—undermining the notion that we're all "in it together" and bound by the same rules.

 • Inequality is also reshaping our politics as wealthier Americans get more adept at turning money into influence—twisting rules to their benefit and escaping punishment when they break the rules.

 • The dramatic upward movement of wealth to top earners has resulted in less wealth for everyone else. Anxiety about money is rife, even among solidly middle-class Americans.

A third consequence of the market's ascendancy is that government's ability to enforce norms of fair play, serving as a "referee" of competition, has been hobbled. Government watchdogs in many areas were disarmed in the '80s and '90s in the name of privatization and deregulation. Extreme laissez-faire thinking has held, foolishly, that the business world can police itself—that the "hidden hand" of market competition will enforce moral behavior and fair outcomes.

Changing Values

Finally the character of Americans has changed. Those values associated with the market hold sway in their most caricatured form: individualism and self-reliance have morphed into selfishness and self-absorption; competitiveness has become social Darwinism; desire for the good life has turned into materialism; aspiration has become envy. There is a growing gap between the life that many Americans want and the life they can afford—a problem that bedevils even those who would seem to have everything. Other values in our culture have been sidelined: belief in community, social responsibility, compassion for the less able or less fortunate. The decline of civic life, famously described by [author] Robert Putnam, has both fueled these changes and been fueled by them. Everywhere the collective spirit needed for a vibrant civil society is struggling to survive in an era where shared goals are out of fashion.

Why have these transformations led to more cheating? There are four key reasons:

New Pressures. In today's competitive economy, where success and job security can't be taken for granted, it's increasingly tempting to leave your ethics at home every morning. Students are cheating more now that getting a good education is a matter of economic life and death. Lawyers are overbilling as they've been pushed to bring in more money for the firm and as it's gotten harder to make partner. Doctors are accepting bribes from drug-makers, as HMOs have squeezed their incomes. The list goes on. You can even see this problem among cabdrivers in some cities. As cabdrivers have gone from salaried workers with steady incomes to "free agents" who rent their taxis and have to hustle to make a living, they've been feeling new pressures to pick up and drop off as many fares as possible every day. And big surprise: They're speeding and running more red lights.

Bigger Rewards for Winning. As the prizes for the winners have increased, people have become more willing to do whatever it takes to be a winner. A CEO will inflate earnings reports to please Wall Street—and increase the value of his stock options by $50 million. An A student will cheat to get the A+ that she believes, correctly, could make the difference between Harvard and a lifetime of big opportunities—or NYU and fewer opportunities. A steady .325 hitter will take steroids to build the muscles needed to be a slugger—and make $12 million a year instead of a mere $3 million. A journalist will fabricate sources in his quest to write as many hit pieces as possible—so that the day arrives sooner rather than later when he can command six-figure book deals and get lucrative lecture gigs. A partner at a top accounting firm will keep quiet and go along as a client cooks the books—in order to protect a mid-six-figure bonus pegged on bringing in and retaining clients, not angering them. . . .

> *The dramatic upward movement of wealth to top earners has resulted in less wealth for everyone else.*

Temptation. Temptations to cheat have increased as safeguards against wrongdoing have grown weaker over two decades of deregulation and attacks on government. Many of the recent instances of greed and investor betrayal on Wall Street, for example, could have been prevented by reforms intended to keep accountants honest—or to ensure the independence of stock analysts, or to stop corporate boards from being packed with cronies, or to keep companies from handing out so many stock options. Reformers tried to enact such measures for years, only to be blocked by powerful special interests and antigovernment zealots. At the same time, federal agencies like the Securities and Exchange Commission (SEC), the IRS, and the Justice Department have been starved of the resources needed to stop white-collar crime. Why not inflate earnings reports if the chances of being prosecuted are next to nil? Why not commit a fraud that nets you $70 million—when a year or two in a Club Fed prison camp is the worst possible punishment? Why not hide your income in an illegal offshore bank account when you know that the IRS is too overwhelmed to bother with you because it actually lost enforcement capacity during the '80s and '90s—even as the number of tax returns increased?

> *Why worry about being thrown out of baseball for using steroids when neither of the major leagues has mandatory drug testing?*

Professional watchdog groups have also been asleep on the job. Why worry about being disbarred for bilking your clients when state bar associations lack the resources or wherewithal to fully investigate much of the misconduct by lawyers reported to them? Why worry about being censured by your state's medical society for taking kickbacks to prescribe certain drugs when those groups are more interested in protecting the interests of doctors than of the general public? Why worry about being thrown out of baseball for using steroids when neither of the major leagues has mandatory drug testing?

Growing temptations to cheat have been all the more seductive given the trumpeted morality of the free market. If competition is good—if even greed is good—than maybe questionable cutthroat behavior is also good. In principle, few Americans embrace the idea that "might makes right." In practice, this idea now flourishes across our society, and much of the new cheating is among those with the highest incomes and social status. The Winning Class's clout inevitably has produced hubris and a sense that the rules governing what Leona Helmsley [one of the richest women in the United States] called "the little people" do not apply to them.

This hubris is only partly founded on the kind of delusions made possible by a culture that imputes moral superiority to those who achieve material success. It is also founded on reality. The Winning Class *can* get away with cheating, if not always then certainly often. And when they do get punished, they often find that it's a cinch to later repair their public image. Rehabilitation in the wake of what scholar David Simon memorably labeled "elite deviance" has become easier in recent decades as bottom-line commercialism has steered the media away from critical inquiry toward a new focus on infotainment, much of it celebrating the accomplishments of the rich and famous.

In short, the Winning Class has every reason to imagine that they live in a moral community of their own making governed by different rules. They do.

> *Middle-class Americans are both insecure and cynical these days.*

Trickle-Down Corruption. What happens when you're an ordinary middle-class person struggling to make ends meet even as you face relentless pressures to emulate the good life you see every day on TV and in magazines? What happens when you think the system is stacked against people like you and you stop believing that the rules are fair? You just might make up your own moral code. Maybe you'll cheat more often on your taxes, anxious to get a leg up financially and also sure that the tax codes wrongly favor the rich. Maybe you'll misuse your expense account at work to afford a few little luxuries that are out of reach on your salary—and you'll justify this on the grounds that the people running your company are taking home huge paychecks while you're making chump change. Maybe you'll lie to the auto insurance company about a claim or about having a teenage driver in the house, convinced that the insurer has jacked up your rates in order to increase their profits—then again, maybe you have nothing against insurance companies but the payments on that flashy new SUV you just had to have are killing you and you're desperate for any kind of relief.

In theory, there is limitless opportunity in America for anyone willing to work hard, and it seemed during the boom of the '90s that everyone could get rich. The reality is that a lot of families actually lost ground during the past two decades. Middle-class Americans are both insecure and cynical these days—a dangerous combination—and many feel besieged by material expectations that are impossible to attain. It shouldn't come as a surprise that more people are leveling the playing field however they see fit. . . .

A Real Conversation About Cheating

A real conversation about cheating is exactly what we need right now. Widespread cheating is undermining some of the most important ideals of American society. The principle of equal opportunity is subverted when those who play by the rules are beaten out by cheaters, as happens every day in academics, sports, business, and other arenas. The belief that hard work is the key to success is mocked when people see, constantly, that success comes faster to those who cut corners. The ideal of equal justice under the law is violated when corporate crooks steal tens of millions of dollars and get slapped on the wrist, while small-time criminals serve long mandatory sentences. . . .

Many of us won't give in to pressures to cheat even when we perceive that everybody else does it. We'll study harder to outdo the cheating students, or train more fanatically to beat the athletes who use drugs, or simply make a point of living our lives in more ethical arenas. But all this means playing by our own rules rather than the prevailing rules, which makes life harder in the process. It means being a hero. It's easier to just go along with the cheating culture. And often, when you're deep inside a system where cheating has been normalized, you can't even see that there are choices between being honest and playing by corrupt rules. . . .

No cultural moment in America lasts forever. The one we have been in for the past quarter century—call it the Market Era—may seem permanent, but it is not. History hasn't ended in the United States or anyplace else.

The trick at moments like these is to make history move faster and change arrive sooner.

12

American Culture Is Obsessed with Violence

Jody M. Roy

Jody M. Roy is an associate professor of communications and chair of the department at Ripon College in Ripon, Wisconsin. She is the author of How We Hate, Why We Hurt: A Guide for Parents, Educators, and Other Everyday Role Models, *and* Love to Hate: America's Obsession with Hatred and Violence, *from which the following viewpoint is excerpted.*

Recent, well-publicized killings, such as the 1999 killing at a Jewish day care center in which a white supremacist shot three children and two employees, reveal how American culture is fascinated with hatred and violence. Although the day care incident and other tragedies received widespread media coverage, Americans remember more about the perpetrators of these crimes than the victims. Criminals are therefore rewarded for their crimes with celebrity. In order to reverse this "culture of death," Americans must first acknowledge that they have willingly been a part of it. Recognizing that hatred is a powerful influence in American culture is necessary to reducing the incidence of violence.

A lone gunman rushes the door of a Jewish community center, opening fire on any person in his path. A group of kindergarten-aged students are the first to encounter him. He does not discriminate—his bullets rip through three of the children, a teenage helper, and an adult employee of the center. While fleeing, he shoots and kills a postal worker.

Two young men wearing long black trench coats enter a suburban high school. It is their high school, filled with their classmates and teachers. They take their time. More than two hours pass before they kill themselves. In those two hours, they kill thirteen others.

All across the nation, small-town residents lock their doors and windows tightly at night, many for the first time in decades. Those living near train tracks suffer a special fear as the so-called Railway Killer eludes police again and again.[1] From Texas to Illinois, the tally of slain bodies continues to climb.

The first report is of a black man shot down in front of his children. Soon after, word crosses the airwaves that a group of Orthodox Jews has been targeted by a drive-by shooter. Almost immediately reporters announce that a car driven by Asian teens also has been hit. One day later a Korean student is killed outside his church. It is the Fourth of July—America is celebrating her national identity: the land of the free and the home of the brave.

A Culture of Death

Being American always has required bravery. The bravery to fight oppression, the bravery to forge a nation from a diverse mix of people, the bravery to embrace democracy not simply as a theory of government but as a way of living. It is only recently that being American has come to mean being brave enough to go to school, brave enough to walk down a public street, brave enough to close your eyes and drift to sleep in your own bed.

> **❝** We don't live in a culture of death, we say, because we despise those who kill. **❞**

The four stories recounted above most probably sound familiar. Sadly, they are real cases of violence that occurred over the course of just four months in 1999. While they were among the most highly reported incidents of violence during that

---

1. The "Railway Killer," Rafael Resendez-Ramirez (aka Angel Maturino Resendez), surrendered in July 1999.

time, the victims constitute only a fraction of the total number of Americans violently attacked by other Americans in any given four-month period.

Although we have long conceived America as the land of the free and the home of the brave, these days we perhaps are reflected more accurately in the phrase used by Pope John Paul II to describe us: a culture of death.

But are we really a culture of death? The phrase "culture of death" seems to imply that we somehow enjoy, even cherish the violence and those who commit it. Surely we do not. Don't we revile these terrible acts? Don't we label the perpetrators "monsters"? Of course we do. The four cases above are the cases of Buford Furrow, the white supremacist who attacked the children in the Jewish Community Center's day camp in California; Eric Harris and Dylan Klebold, the Columbine High School students from Littleton, Colorado, who committed the most lethal of the string of school shootings in the 1990s; Angel Maturino Resendez, among the most recent serial killers to terrorize Americans; and Benjamin Smith, the disenchanted university student who briefly affiliated himself with the World Church of the Creator and later rampaged through a two-day killing spree in Illinois and Indiana.

> *We finally have to admit that we are, as a country, obsessed with hatred.*

We recognize all these killers as bad people, even evil people. We don't live in a culture of death, we say, because we despise those who kill.

But it is unlikely that we can name even one of their victims. What do we know about the three children attending day camp? Their teenage helper? The employee of the center? The postal worker? Any of the twelve students who will never graduate from Columbine High School? The teacher who will never again teach? We are unlikely to remember the name of the woman killed by the tracks in a small Texas town or the names of any of the other seven people who lost their lives to the Railway Killer or the black man whose children watched him die or the Orthodox Jewish men or the Asian teens or the Korean student.

We reward the violent with one of our most valued commodities: celebrity. We do not celebrate the innocent. We usu-ally don't even remember their names. When we remember them at all, we remember only that they were killed. But the killers we remember. And by remembering them, we write our own legacy. America at the turn of the millennium no doubt will be judged by future generations as we ourselves judge the past: by the records we leave of those who emerge from the masses to become *known.*

Reining in the Violence

The question then becomes, how do we escape the culture of death? How do we rein in the violence that has become a defin-ing characteristic of America? Individually and as a society, we finally have to admit that we are, as a country, obsessed with ha-tred. Although we like to romanticize it, our fascination with hatred is not romantic. It is a seedy flirtation, an illicit affair. We publicly profess our commitment to compassion and peace, yet we carry on with hatred and violence on the side. In recent decades, we've become ever more brazen, parading our liaison out in public for all the world—including our children—to wit-ness. Should it really surprise us, then, that some of our children, born as they were into the midst of our flirtation with hatred, lash out violently? Should we be shocked that our longtime ob-session finally spawned a culture of death? Of course not. We should be surprised, shocked, and even appalled only at our own foolishness in believing we somehow could sustain a long-term fling with hatred and violence without compromising the in-tegrity of our commitment to compassion and peace.

How then do we begin to change? We first must admit that we have been willing parties to this affair. No one forced it on us. While hatred and violence can be seductive, we ultimately choose and keep choosing to give in to their temptations. By fi-nally, fully owning up to the fact that we have been willing par-ties in this obsessive relationship, we empower ourselves to end it. As we all know, it only takes one side leaving to end a love affair.

I began thinking of America's relationship with hatred and violence as an obsession several years ago. As a professor of communication, I have focused my scholarly research for more than a decade on the question, "How do people become per-suaded to hate other people?" From my formal studies of orga-nized hate groups to my informal discussions with students about their reactions to violence in the media, I've come to realize that we Americans like to accuse other people of hating and being violent, but nearly all of us, myself included, harbor a fascination with hatred and violence. We are quick to point the finger of blame at killers, hate group members, even rap artists for promoting violence, yet we have a voracious appetite for both real and fictional stories about the very people we say are dangerous.

> *While hatred and violence can be seductive, we ultimately choose and keep choosing to give in to their temptations.*

My thoughts about our relationship with hatred and violence crystallized in 1999 when news broke of the Columbine massacre. I happened to be at home that afternoon and, like millions of others, watched the live coverage of a mass murder in progress. I couldn't take my eyes off the television. "How could this happen?" I asked myself. "What has our world come to?" The news reporters echoed my thoughts, asking "Why? Why?," as we all watched video of a bleeding teenage boy hanging out of a window as SWAT team members dared a rescue attempt.

Having spent more than ten years studying the most extreme incarnations of hatred and violence, I am more jaded than most people. Over the years, I have developed a necessary survival skill, the ability to distance myself from my research subject. My scholarly detachment enabled me to watch coverage of earlier school shootings—Jonesboro, Pearl, Paducah, among others—as little more than cases-in-point of established academic theories. So what was it that made Columbine unique for me? Was it the live coverage? No. Was it the sheer number of victims? No. Columbine was unique for me because as I sat on the edge of my seat watching live coverage of a mass murder, I cradled my infant daughter in my arms. Columbine was the first time I encountered my research area not just as an academic but as a parent. . . .

As a result of the events of September 11, 2001, many people are anxious to participate in [conversations about how hatred and violence affect us all]. The terrorist attacks on the United States and the ensuing international "war on terrorism" have taken center stage in conversations, as well as in the American cultural consciousness. On some levels September 11, 2001, and its aftermath have changed most Americans profoundly.

Yet, as attention has narrowed onto threats from abroad, Americans have risked losing sight of the forms of home-grown hatred that so recently gave rise to the rash of school shootings, the Oklahoma City bombing, and other horrific acts of violence. The hatred that inspires such violence has not left America. If anything, the "war on terrorism" provides new impetus and outlets for hatred and violence here in the United States. For example, within less than a week of September 11, more than two hundred people perceived to be Middle Eastern or Moslem were the victims of hate crimes in the United States; two were killed. Additionally, the fear and anger nearly all Americans have felt since September 11 make people, individually and collectively, more vulnerable than they have been in decades to the seductive powers of hatred. . . .

If we hope ever to live in an era free of hatred and violence, we must not allow our legitimate concerns about international terrorism to distract us from equally legitimate concerns about the persistent reality of hatred violence within our own culture. . . .

Of course, we cannot dive into a consideration of this subject [the problems of hatred] without first pausing to define hatred itself. A dictionary offers synonyms for "hatred" such as "repugnance," "detestation," and "abhorrence." Those terms don't really help us grasp the scope of "hatred." Hatred is complex and dynamic. It is at once an emotion, a passion, a force, a cultural commodity, a motivation, a value, a status symbol, and a source of power. Hatred is not a static thing, an object we can bottle up and label. Rather, hatred exists between and among us. Hatred is not simply a term denoting a feeling humans sometimes experience but a filter through which we humans at times choose to see the world and be in the world. We give hatred life in our thoughts and words. And when we fail to realize the power of those thoughts and words to influence our behavior, we invite the kind of violence that led Pope John Paul II to label America at the dawn of the new millennium a "culture of death."

Organizations to Contact

The editors have compiled the following list of organizations concerned with the issues debated in this book. The descriptions are derived from materials provided by the organizations. All have publications or information available for interested readers. The list was compiled on the date of publication of the present volume; the information provided here may change. Be aware that many organizations take several weeks or longer to respond to inquiries, so allow as much time as possible.

American Atheists
PO Box 5733, Parsippany, NJ 07054-6733
(908) 276-7300 • fax: (908) 276-7402
e-mail: info@atheists.org • Web site: www.atheists.org

American Atheists is an educational organization dedicated to the complete and absolute separation of church and state. It opposes religious involvement such as prayer and religious clubs in public schools. The organization's purpose is to stimulate freedom of thought and inquiry concerning religious beliefs and practices. It publishes the monthly *American Atheist Newsletter.*

American Civil Liberties Union (ACLU)
125 Broad St., 18th Fl., New York, NY 10004
(212) 549-2500 • fax: (212) 549-2646
Web site: www.aclu.org

The ACLU is a national organization that works to defend Americans' civil rights as guaranteed by the U.S. Constitution. It works to establish equality before the law, regardless of race, color, sexual orientation, or national origin. The ACLU publishes and distributes policy statements, pamphlets, and the semiannual newsletter *Civil Liberties Alert.*

Americans for Religious Liberty (ARL)
PO Box 6656, Silver Spring, MD 20916
(301) 260-2988 • fax: (301) 260-2989
e-mail: arlinc@erols.com • Web site: www.arlinc.org

ARL is an educational organization that works to preserve religious, intellectual, and personal freedom in a secular democracy. It advocates the strict separation of church and state. ARL publishes numerous pamphlets on church/state issues and the quarterly newsletter *Voice of Reason.*

Cato Institute
1000 Massachusetts Ave. NW, Washington, DC 20001-5403
(202) 842-0200 • fax: (202) 842-3490
e-mail: cato@cato.org • Web site: www.cato.org

The Cato Institute is a libertarian public policy research foundation dedicated to limiting the control of government and protecting individual liberties. It offers numerous publications on public policy issues, including the triennial *Cato Journal*, the bimonthly newsletter *Cato Policy Report*, and the quarterly magazine *Regulation*.

Center for Media and Public Affairs (CMPA)
2100 L St. NW, Suite 300, Washington, DC 20037
(202) 223-2942 • fax: (202) 872-4014
e-mail: mail@cmpa.com • Web site: www.cmpa.com

CMPA is a research organization that studies the media treatment of social and political affairs. It uses surveys to measure the media's influence on public opinion. It publishes the monthly *Media Monitor*, the monograph *A Day of Television Violence*, and various other books, articles, and monographs.

Center for Media Literacy
3101 Ocean Park Blvd., Suite 200, Santa Monica, CA 90405
(310) 581-0260 • fax: (310) 581-0270
e-mail: cml@medialit.org • Web site: www.medialit.org

The center is a media education organization. It seeks to give the public power over the media by fostering media literacy. It publishes the quarterly *Media & Values*.

Christian Coalition of America (CC)
PO Box 37030, Washington, DC 20013-7030
(202) 424-2630 • fax: (202) 479-4260
e-mail: coalition@cc.org • Web site: www.cc.org

Founded by evangelist Pat Robertson, the coalition is a grassroots political organization of Christian fundamentalists working to stop what it believes is the moral decay of government. The coalition seeks to elect moral legislators and opposes extramarital sex and comprehensive drug and sex education. Its publications include the monthly newsletter *The Religious Right Watch* and the monthly tabloid *Christian American*.

Coalition on Human Needs (CHN)
1102 Connecticut Ave. NW, Suite 910, Washington, DC 20036
(202) 223-2532 • fax: (202) 233-2538
e-mail: chn@chn.org • Web site: www.chn.org

The coalition is a federal advocacy organization concerned with federal budget and tax policy, housing education, health care, and public assistance. It lobbies for adequate federal funding for welfare, Medicaid, and other social services. Its publications include *How the Poor Would Remedy Poverty* and the bimonthly newsletter *Insight/Action*.

Concerned Women for America (CWA)
1015 Fifteenth St. NW, Suite 1100, Washington, DC 20005
(202) 488-7000 • fax: (202) 488-0806
Web site: www.cwfa.org

CWA's purpose is to preserve, protect, and promote traditional Judeo-Christian values through education, legislative action, and other activities. It is concerned with creating an environment that is conducive to building strong families and raising healthy children. CWA publishes the monthly *Family Voice*, which periodically addresses issues such as abortion and promoting sexual abstinence in schools.

Eagle Forum
PO Box 618, Alton, IL 62002
(618) 462-5415 • fax: (618) 462-8909
e-mail: eagle@eagleforum.org • Web site: www.eagleforum.org

Eagle Forum is a Christian group that promotes morality and traditional family values as revealed through the Bible. It opposes many facets of public education and liberal government. The forum publishes the monthly *Phyllis Schlafly Report* and a periodic newsletter.

Family Research Council (FRC)
801 G St. NW, Washington, DC 20001
(202) 393-2100 • fax: (202) 393-2134
e-mail: corrdept@frc.org • Web site: www.frc.org

The council is a research, resource, and education organization that promotes the traditional family, which it defines as a group of people bound by marriage, blood, or adoption. It opposes schools' tolerance of homosexuality and school condom distribution programs. The council publishes numerous reports from a conservative perspective. These publications include the monthly newsletter *Washington Watch*, the bimonthly journal *Family Policy*, and *Free to Be Family*, a report that focuses on children and families.

Heritage Foundation
214 Massachusetts Ave. NE, Washington, DC 20002-4999
(202) 546-4400 • fax: (202) 546-8328
e-mail: info@heritage.org • Web site: www.heritage.org

The Heritage Foundation is a conservative public policy research institute that advocates free-market economics and limited government. Its publications include the monthly *Policy Review*, the Backgrounder series of occasional papers, and the Heritage Lectures series.

Morality in Media (MIM)
475 Riverside Dr., Suite 239, New York, NY 10115
(212) 870-3222 • fax: (212) 870-2765
e-mail: mim@moralityinmedia.org
Web site: www.moralityinmedia.org

MIM opposes what it considers to be indecency in broadcasting—especially the broadcasting of pornography. It works to educate and organize the public in support of strict decency laws, and it has launched an annual "turn off TV day" to protest offensive television programming. The group publishes the *Morality in Media Newsletter* and the handbook *TV: The World's Greatest Mind-Bender*.

National Coalition Against Censorship (NCAC)
275 Seventh Ave., New York, NY 10001
(212) 807-6222 • fax: (212) 807-6245
e-mail: ncac@ncac.org • Web site: www.ncac.org

NCAC is an alliance of organizations committed to defending freedom of thought, inquiry, and expression by engaging in public education and advocacy on national and local levels. It publishes periodic reports and the monthly *Censorship News*.

National Organization for Women (NOW)
733 Fifteenth St. NW, Washington, DC 20005
(202) 268-8669 • fax: (202) 785-8576
e-mail: now@now.org • Web site: www.now.org

NOW is one of the largest and most influential feminist organizations in the United States. It seeks to end prejudice and discrimination against women in all areas of life. It lobbies legislatures for more equitable laws and works to educate and inform the public on women's issues. NOW publishes the bimonthly tabloid *NOW Times*, policy statements, and articles.

People for the American Way (PFAW)
2000 M St. NW, Suite 400, Washington, DC 20036
(202) 467-4999 • fax: (202) 293-2672
e-mail: pfaw@pfaw.org • Web site: www.pfaw.org

PFAW works to increase tolerance and respect for America's diverse cultures, religions, and values such as freedom of expression. It distributes educational materials, leaflets, and brochures and publishes the quarterly *Press Clips*, a collection of newspaper articles concerning censorship.

Progressive Policy Institute (PPI)
600 Pennsylvania Ave. SE, Suite 400, Washington, DC 20003
(202) 546-0001 • fax: (202) 544-5014
Web site: www.ppionline.org

PPI is a public policy research organization that strives to develop alternatives to the traditional debate between liberals and conservatives. It advocates economic policies designed to stimulate broad upward mobility and social policies designed to liberate the poor from poverty and dependence. The institute publishes the book *Building the Bridge: Ten Big Ideas to Transform America*.

Rockford Institute
928 N. Main St., Rockford, IL 61103-7061
(815) 964-5053 • fax: (815) 964-9403
e-mail: info@rockfordinstitute.org
Web site: www.chroniclesmagazine.org

The institute works to return America to Judeo-Christian values and supports traditional roles for men and women. It stresses the advantages of two-parent families as the best way to raise children. Its Center on Religion and Society advocates a more public role for religion and religious values in American life. The institute's publications include the monthly periodical *Family in America*, the monthly *Religion and Society Report*, and the quarterly newsletter *Main Street Memorandum*.

Bibliography

Books

William J. Bennett	*The Broken Hearth: Reversing the Moral Collapse of the American Family*. New York: Broadway, 2003.
Tammy Bruce	*The Death of Right and Wrong: Exposing the Left's Assault on Our Culture and Values*. Roseville, CA: Forum, 2003.
Tammy Bruce and Laura C. Schlessinger	*The New Thought Police: Inside the Left's Assault on Free Speech and Free Minds*. New York: Three Rivers, 2003.
Patrick J. Buchanan	*The Death of the West: How Dying Populations and Immigrant Invasions Imperil Our Country and Civilization*. New York: St. Martin's, 2002.
David Callahan	*The Cheating Culture: Why More Americans Are Doing Wrong to Get Ahead*. Orlando, FL: Harcourt, 2004.
John DeGraaf et al.	*Affluenza: The All-Consuming Epidemic*. San Francisco: Berrett-Koehler, 2002.
Barry Glassner	*The Culture of Fear: Why Americans Are Afraid of the Wrong Things*. New York: Basic Books, 2000.
Herbert London	*Decade of Denial: A Snapshot of America in the 1990s*. Lanham, MD: Lexington, 2001.
John Harmon McElroy	*American Beliefs: What Keeps a Big Country and a Diverse People United*. Chicago: Ivan R. Dee, 1999.
David Murray	*It Ain't Necessarily So: How the Media Remake Our Picture of Reality*. New York: Penguin, 2002.
Jedediah Purdy	*Being America: Liberty, Commerce, and Violence in an American World*. New York: Knopf, 2003.
Jonathan Rieder and Stephen Steinlight	*The Fractious Nation? Unity and Division in Contemporary American Life*. Berkeley: University of California Press, 2003.
Jody M. Roy	*Love to Hate: America's Obsession with Hatred and Violence*. New York: Columbia University Press, 2002.
Michael Savage	*The Enemy Within: Saving America from the Liberal Assault on Our Schools, Faith, and Military*. Nashville: WND, 2003.

Michael Shermer   *Why People Believe Weird Things: Pseudoscience, Superstition, and Other Confusions of Our Time.* New York: Owl, 2002.

Periodicals

Ronald Berenbeim   "What Is Ethical? An American View," *Vital Speeches of the Day*, July 1, 2002.

Gerard V. Bradley   "Stand and Fight: Don't Take Gay Marriage Lying Down," *National Review*, July 28, 2003.

Robert J. Bresler   "Cultural Decline and Political Dependency," *USA Today*, September 2001.

Forrest Church   "The American Creed: U.S. Values Rest Historically on a Spiritual Foundation Grounded in Nature," *Nation*, September 16, 2002.

Randy Cohen   "The Politics of Ethics: By Identifying Ethics with Civic Virtue, We Create an Ethics of the Left," *Nation*, April 8, 2002.

Marty Dannenfelser   "The Culture War Can Be Won with Perseverance," *Insight on the News*, March 29, 1999.

Thom Hartmann   "Have We Already Played the Game and Lost?" *Tikkun*, November 1999.

Gerald F. Kreyche   "Are Younger People Worse Off than Their Parents?" *USA Today*, September 2003.

Michael Linton   "The Blight of Cultural Rights," *First Things*, June 2001.

Jerry L. Martin   "Restoring American Cultural Institutions," *Society*, January/February 1999.

Lee Siegel   "On Television—Reality in America," *New Republic*, June 23, 2003.

Woody West   "Cacophony About the American Character," *Insight on the News*, February 2, 2004.

Index